SMALL HELPINGS

BY ANNABEL KARMEL

SMALL HELPINGS

BY ANNABEL KARMEL

*A complete guide to feeding
babies, toddlers and young children*

COLE GROUP

For my children
Nicholas, Lara and Scarlett

© 1995 Cole Publishing Group, Inc.

This edition published by Cole Publishing Group, Inc.
1330 N. Dutton Ave., Ste 103
Santa Rosa, CA 95401
by arrangement with
BBC Books, a division of BBC Worldwide Ltd.

Original English Language Version published by BBC Books, a division of BBC Worldwide
Ltd., © Annabel Karmel 1994

ISBN 1-56426-077-1
Library of Congress Cataloging in Process

Designed by Annette Peppis
Illustrations by Sally Davies
Back cover photograph by Stanley Lenman

Printed and bound in Great Britain

Although every effort has been made at the time of publication to guarantee the accuracy of information sources and technical data, readers must assume responsibility for selection and use of suppliers and supplies. The information contained in this book is intended as a general guide to nutritious cooking for children and is not intended to replace the sound advice of your child's pediatrician or other healthcare professional. The reader should consult a healthcare professional before embarking on any major dietary changes. Because of the risk of bacterial contamination, health professionals do not recommend feeding raw or lightly cooked eggs to babies and young children.

CONTENTS

INTRODUCTION

I am the mother of three children under the age of five – Nicholas, Lara and Scarlett – and like any mother I wanted to give them the best possible start in life.

Young children are most in need of a nutritious diet for their growing bodies; the quality of food fed to babies is critical to their health not only as babies but also later in life. Research has shown that a poor diet in early life can lead to bad health and impaired mental development in adulthood. Recent research by a team led by Professor Alan Lucas in Cambridge, England, suggests that feeding breast milk rather than formula milk to premature babies for as short a period as four weeks at a time of maximum growth can influence IQ. Almost 25 percent of young children in the US and UK suffer from a deficiency in iron. Iron deficiency anemia in young children can lead to permanently impaired mental development. Coronary heart disease is a leading cause of death in the US and UK, and there is little doubt that the disease process is often related to diet and can begin in childhood.

We are coming close to the point where it can be proved that early feeding influences do matter to long-term health. Babies cannot choose for themselves what they eat, and young children do not understand the importance of good nutrition, so we as parents must take on that responsibility. As attitudes towards food are established in childhood it is vitally important to establish a healthy diet from an early age.

The long lists of nutritional information on commercial baby foods look impressive, but water and thickeners are often used to bulk up the ingredients and unnecessary additives are put in some products. There is absolutely no doubt – and baby food manufacturers will be the first to agree – that nothing is better for your baby than freshly prepared food; making baby food yourself also is cheaper than buying it in jars. There is such a lot of mystique surrounding baby foods that, when Nicholas was born, I thought that a jar of applesauce had some special ingredients and was somehow better for my baby than if I cooked and puréed apples myself.

I know that many mothers feel they just don't have the time or the required skills, but making baby food at home is simple. You don't need lots of special equipment, and in just a couple of hours you can prepare a whole month's food supply for your baby.

I have written this book on the premise that a recipe has to be easy or a busy parent won't make it. All the recipes in this book can be prepared without spending hours in the kitchen, and all use fresh, natural ingredients. The emphasis is on cooking for the whole family; many of the purées I made for my babies were so tasty that I often made extra-large quantities and served the rest of the family a delicious soup for supper!

Throughout this book there are many handy timesaving tips and lots of advice for all stages of your child's development to get you through the difficult times. Believe me, I've been there – Nicholas went through a stage of just not eating; Lara (my little junk food addict) would eat only if all her food were covered with a blanket of tomato ketchup; and Scarlett likes to eat everything in sight, even if it's not food – but then she's only one!

There are recipes for all occasions, from delicious everyday meals, healthy snacks and lunch boxes to birthday party fare. Nearly all the recipes can be frozen so that you can have a ready supply of healthy, homemade convenience foods in your freezer.

I hope this book will prove a treasure trove of ideas when it comes to feeding your child and will help to establish a healthy eating pattern for the rest of her life. You will be reassured to know that every recipe has been tested by a panel of small people who were never hesitant to show me exactly what they thought if they weren't impressed!

Basic Nutrition

Government health recommendations tell us we should cut down on fats (especially saturated ones), added sugars and salt. It should be possible to achieve the recommended low-fat, low-sugar diet by the age of five years. This goal has been taken into consideration when devising the recipes – all use minimum amounts of sugar, fat and salt. As a general rule, though, it's useful to bear the following guidelines in mind when preparing food for your child.

◆ SALT: Don't add extra salt at the table. Use none or very small amounts in recipes. Try using herbs for flavor instead.

◆ FAT: Butter contains mainly saturated fat; polyunsaturated margarines or oils can be used in the recipes if preferred. For older children low-fat milk can be used in place of whole milk and yogurt or crème fraîche in place of cream.

◆ SUGAR: Try to sweeten with pure fruit juice as there is less chance of over-sweetening. Don't use artificial sweeteners in foods or drinks.

Iron

The most important nutrient for babies and toddlers is iron. Iron deficiency is perhaps the most common nutritional problem in young children in the West and will leave your child feeling tired and run-down. As I mentioned in my Introduction, iron is an important factor in brain development, and an early deficiency in iron may have a profound influence on learning development. On average, babies are born with sufficient iron reserves in their liver to meet their needs only until they double their birth weight, or for approximately the first six months of life.

The iron in breast milk can be easily absorbed, and infant and follow-up formulas also contain good quantities of iron. It is therefore best to continue with one of these for the first year.

It is important to select iron-rich weaning foods even if your baby is given iron-fortified milk in the first year. Introducing the right diet early on should encourage your baby to include these foods in his daily diet as he grows older, especially once he is drinking ordinary cow's milk, which is a poor source of iron.

Some forms of iron are not as well absorbed into our bodies as others. Because iron in foods of animal origin is better absorbed than iron in foods of plant origin, your child will benefit more from the iron in red meat than by eating large quantities of iron-enriched breakfast cereal. Liver and other organ meats are the richest natural sources of iron. Liver is an excellent food for young babies; it is easily digested and makes a very smooth purée. Liver pâté, however, should not be given to babies under a year because of the danger of listeriosis, a serious bacterial disease.

Foods that provide a good source of iron:
liver
red meat
egg yolk
kidney beans
lentils
dark green leafy vegetables like spinach and beet greens
dried fruit, especially dried apricots and prunes
whole-grain cereals (many of these are also fortified with iron)
oily fish like mackerel or salmon

Iron-rich foods for babies over six months:
puréed liver and potato
puréed chicken and chicken livers
puréed vegetables with sieved egg yolk
lentil and vegetable purée
dried apricots with iron-fortified baby rice and milk
puréed spinach and potato

Ideas for snacks that are rich in iron:
chopped liver and egg sandwiches
egg salad sandwiches
peanut butter and raisin sandwiches★
dried apricots★
prunes★
dried figs★
turkey chunks (dark meat)

Iron present in vegetables, cereals and other nonanimal forms is better absorbed by our bodies if vitamin C is consumed at the same meal. Good sources of vitamin C are fresh fruits and vegetables, particularly citrus fruits. Some infant cereals are fortified with iron, and it is a good idea to mix fruit and vegetable purées rich in vitamin C with them. This will also help to thicken some of your purées.

★ *Eat with a good vitamin C source, e.g., oranges or cantaloupe, to improve absorption of the iron they contain.*

CALCIUM

MILK AND MILK PRODUCTS

Dairy foods provide the best source of calcium, which is important for healthy bones and teeth. Most babies have a diet based on milk for the first year, but you may not know that adolescents need even more calcium than younger children and adults. That's because calcium is a major component of bones, and almost half our adult bone mass is formed during adolescence. Make sure that your child gets the calcium she needs between the ages of 11 and 18. Two thirds of a pint (10 fl oz or 1¼ cups) of milk a day provides adequate calcium between one and five years.

The following foods contain the same calcium as 10 fl oz (1¼ cups) of milk:

1½ oz	*Cheddar cheese*
2 oz	*Mozzarella cheese*
7 oz	*yogurt*
9 oz	*baked custard*
2⅓ oz	*tofu*
1 lb	*cottage cheese*
9 oz	*ice cream*
2 oz	*sardines*

FATS

Children are very active and need energy-giving food. However, their stomachs are small so meals should not be too bulky. Fat is important as it provides the most concentrated supply of energy and thus reduces the bulk of the diet. Young children need a higher proportion of fat in their diet than adults do to get the energy they need from their food. Remember that babies should be rather fat until they start using up a reasonable amount of energy in walking (around 18 months). Nature's intended food, breast milk, contains about 50 percent fat and is better absorbed by infants than the fat in milks of other mammals. The big question is, which are the best types of fat for our children?

There are two main types of fat: **saturated** and **unsaturated**. Saturated fats (in butter, cheese, milk and other dairy products, and in meat and meat products like lard and meat drippings) tend to raise blood cholesterol levels and increase the risk of heart disease. Unsaturated fats (in oils of vegetable origin, like olive oil, and in polyunsaturated margarine and oily fish) tend to decrease cholesterol levels. However, the risk of heart disease in later life resulting from eating saturated fat in the first five years of life is negligible compared to a nutritional deficiency due to a marked reduction in dairy fat, so there is no need to restrict foods like cheese and other dairy products. But it is best to give lean meat and get into the habit of using unsaturated fats for cooking.

Whole milk is also an exception to the guidelines on saturated fats as children under the age of two should certainly drink whole milk and not skimmed milk. The essential vitamins A and D, present in whole milk, are fat-soluble and therefore lost in the skimming process. Low-fat dairy products are also not appropriate for very young children. Within a balanced diet low-fat milk is all right from two to three years.

CARBOHYDRATES

Carbohydrates and fats provide our body with the main source of energy. There are two types of carbohydrate: **sugar** and **starch**.

Most nutritionists would like to see bread and other cereals and vegetables, which are all forms of starch, provide an increasing proportion of our carbohydrate intake. Unlike most starches, sugar has no nutritional value other than providing energy and it is the major cause of dental decay in children's teeth. Whenever possible, children should take sugar in a natural form (you can sweeten foods by adding fruit juice) and not in refined products like cookies and cakes. Don't be misled: honey is no better than sugar, and glucose, dextrose and sucrose are simply other names for sugar.

EAT MORE

EAT LESS

STARCH	
whole-grain breakfast cereals	*refined, sugar-coated breakfast cereals*
whole-grain bread and flour	*white bread and white flour*
brown rice	*white rice*
beans and lentils	*cookies and cakes*
pasta	

SUGAR	
fruit	*soft drinks*
vegetables	*packaged gelatin desserts*
	sugar and honey

PROTEIN

Most of us eat more protein than we need, yet protein deficiency is almost unheard of in the US and UK. Your baby doesn't need large amounts, especially while he is still having a lot of milk, which is a good source of protein.

Proteins are needed for the growth and repair of our bodies and are made up of different amino acids. Some foods – meat, poultry, fish, dairy products, including cheese and yogurt, and soy beans – are "complete" proteins and contain all the amino acids that are essential to our bodies. Other foods like whole-grain cereals, bread, legumes, nuts and seeds, enriched pastas, brown rice and peanut butter are "incomplete" proteins, which provide some of the protein elements essential for good nutrition. These foods are also good because they tend to be inexpensive.

WATER

When my son Nicholas was a baby, the last drink I thought of giving him was water. Millions of dollars worth of baby drinks are sold each year, and I suppose I was fooled into thinking that all the soothing herbal teas and vitamin-enriched fruit drinks were better for him. It was only when I examined their contents more closely that I discovered that most of these baby drinks were no better than sugary water.

Milk provides all the nutrients that young babies need, and offering other drinks may well reduce your baby's appetite for milk. Unless the weather is particularly hot, many babies need drink nothing other than milk.

As your baby grows older and eats more solid food, his need for water will become greater. It is a good idea to get your baby accustomed to water at an early age; once he has acquired a taste for sweet fruit drinks and herbal teas, it may be too late. A good idea is to give water when you first introduce a cup (around 8 months). The novelty of the cup may encourage your baby to drink water.

Bottles should not be made up with mineral water: it is not bacteriologically safe unless boiled, and some mineral waters contain high levels of sodium and phosphate. Boiled, cooled tap water is best; it usually contains fluoride, which helps to strengthen teeth.

VITAMINS

If a baby or child is eating a good balanced diet, there is no need for vitamin supplements. My opinion is that these are given more for the parent's peace of mind than for the benefit of the child.

Some nutrients can be stored in the body

— these are mainly the fat-soluble vitamins A, D, E and K. They have to be eaten only once or twice a week. Other nutrients, particularly the water-soluble vitamins of the B group and vitamin C, are not really stored and should be eaten every day.

Some vitamins (and minerals) can be lost during cooking if you are not careful. Vitamin C is destroyed by heat, so don't overcook vegetables. Some of the B vitamins can leak out of the food into the cooking water, so it will help if you use some of the cooking liquid to make a sauce or gravy (for example, a cheese sauce if you are cooking cauliflower). Try to give your child raw vegetables sometimes. Otherwise it is best to steam them.

If you have no fresh vegetables or fruits, then the next best choice is the frozen variety. In fact, some frozen foods that are frozen immediately after they are picked can be even fresher than foods that have been kept in your refrigerator for several days (see page 69).

WHAT MAKES A BALANCED DIET?

A healthy diet for adults isn't always quite right for growing children. Children need a lot of energy-giving foods as they have small stomachs and so can only eat small amounts of food at a time. They need food that is high in energy without being too filling, otherwise they'll fill up on bulky high-fiber foods before they've eaten enough calories and nutrients. There are **four** basic food groups that are important to your child's diet from which you should try to include roughly a certain number of portions each day:

◆ MILK AND DAIRY PRODUCTS
The recommended daily number of servings is related to the age of the individual.

Babies up to 6 months: 4 bottles (8 fl oz each) each day.
6 to 9 months: at least 1 pint each day.
Children: 3 servings per day.
Teenagers: 4 servings per day.

1 serving = 5 fl oz or 1 cup (see page 10 for equivalents).

◆ FRUITS AND VEGETABLES
Four or more servings per day (preferably one serving vitamin C-rich fruit each day and a dark green leafy or a yellow vegetable every other day).

◆ MEAT AND MEAT ALTERNATIVES
Two or more servings per day.

◆ BREADS AND CEREALS

Four or more servings of whole-grain or enriched breads or cereals per day.

When solids are first introduced, you don't need to worry about a balanced diet as your baby will be getting everything she needs from milk. However, good habits should start early, so around 6–8 months try to work towards giving your baby a properly balanced diet.

MILK AND MILK PRODUCTS

Milk and milk products provide calcium, protein and vitamin D. However, soft cheeses such as Brie are not recommended for babies under a year because of the danger of listeriosis. Babies need whole-milk dairy products to get the energy they need, and if your child isn't very keen on drinking milk, then yogurt, cheese, creamed soup or even quality ice creams are all good sources of milk. Remember, though, that cow's milk is a poor source of iron, so don't let your child drink so much milk that he has no appetite for solids, which will provide iron in his diet. The recommended maximum amount for children over one year is 1 pint daily.

FRUITS AND VEGETABLES

These foods are high in carbohydrates and contribute fiber and vitamins A, C and E to the diet as well as important minerals like potassium, calcium and iron. Try to include fruits or vegetables that are a good source of vitamin C and A every day. One of the best things you can do for your children is to get them interested in fruits and vegetables at an early age.

VITAMIN C FOODS

Citrus fruits, cantaloupe, apricots, kiwi fruit, papaya, cauliflower, Brussels sprouts, cabbage, tomatoes, peppers, berries.

VITAMIN A FOODS

Sweet potato, carrots, cantaloupe, apricots, peas, broccoli, dark green leafy vegetables.

MEAT AND MEAT ALTERNATIVES

Meat provides protein, iron, zinc and vitamin B_{12}. Even without red meat most children eating a good varied diet will get the protein they need from alternative sources like chicken, fish, eggs, seeds, grains, tofu, legumes and nuts, even peanut butter. Eggs are still the most complete source of protein in our diet. Just one egg provides half of the protein needs of a two- to three-year-old child. Egg yolks are packed with calcium and phosphorus for building and maintaining strong bones and teeth, and are a good source of iron. However, soft-cooked eggs should not be given to babies under a year because of the danger of salmonella.

Red meat and liver provide the best source of iron for your child. If your child is drinking a lot of cow's milk and eating mainly foods low in iron then iron deficiency anemia may occur. See the section on iron (page 8) to help you choose foods and recipes that are good sources of iron.

Red meat has been branded by some health gurus as unhealthy, yet lean red meat with all the fat trimmed off contains only five percent fat. In moderation, red meat is very nutritious for your child.

BREADS AND CEREALS

These foods provide iron, niacin, thiamine and fiber. Choose whole-grain and enriched breads and cereals for your child – whole-wheat bread and pasta, brown rice, and cereal. Niacin and thiamine are both B vitamins, vital for energy and emotional balance and important for hair, skin and nails.

Recently there has been a lot of concern over the lack of fiber in the Western diet, but in the case of babies and young children, care needs to be taken not to include too much fiber. High-fiber foods tend to be bulky and young children may feel full before they can eat enough to get sufficient nutrients and energy. Some types of fiber, like wheat bran, also contain substances that interfere with the body's absorption of vitamins and minerals. So choose foods like whole-grain bread and breakfast cereals in your child's diet but avoid foods with added fiber and don't add bran to young children's food.

VEGETARIAN AND VEGAN DIETS

Parents who follow a vegetarian diet are often concerned that this might be unsuitable for their baby. In fact a vegetarian diet that includes egg, milk and dairy products is a perfectly good diet for babies. All animal protein, including egg and milk, is a high-quality protein. Cereal and vegetable protein has a lower quality, although the protein from peas, beans, nuts and lentils is almost as good as animal protein.

In order for your child to get a high-quality protein at each meal, you should include some dairy food – it need be only a small quantity – or combine different nonanimal proteins together (for example, cereal and vegetable protein at the same meal, such as peas and baby rice. See Rice is nice (page 75) or Tasty tofu (page 78).

A vegan diet, excluding all animal foods, may pose some difficulties for a young baby. Large quantities of bulky cereals, vegetables and legumes need to be eaten in order to provide enough nutrients, and young babies are not able to consume these large amounts of food.

Of course if the baby is being breast-fed then it will be getting very good quality protein from its mother's milk. After breast-feeding has stopped then it is advisable for vegan babies to take a specially adapted infant soy formula (adult soy milks are not suitable). At least a pint of this should be taken up to the age of at least one year and preferably beyond this.

One particular B vitamin is found only in animal foods – vitamin B_{12}. It should be present in breast milk and the special soy formulas also contain plenty. But if these foods are not included in the diet then a supplement needs to be given. Vegetarians and in particular vegan babies can also suffer a deficiency in iron. Some vegetable foods such as beans and dark green leafy vegetables contain iron, but you need to give a vitamin C-rich food (e.g., orange segments) with them as this helps absorption.

FOOD ALLERGIES

Everybody is equipped with an immune system and when a foreign body like a measles virus gets inside us, our body manufactures a substance called an antibody to beat off the invader. This defense works well to fight off disease; however, sometimes our body might identify a fairly harmless substance like a particular food as being a foreign substance and create large amounts of antibodies. This can result in unpleasant side effects. A **food reaction** is generally short-lived and not the same as a true **food allergy,** which involves the body's immune system. The symptoms of food intolerance can manifest in several different ways: vomiting, diarrhea, abdominal pain, nausea, asthma, eczema and swelling. The only treatment available for a true food allergy is to avoid the problem food.

There is an enormous amount of anxiety about food allergies, which can make parents nervous when it comes to feeding their babies. However, unless there is a family history, food allergies affect only a very small minority of babies. Food intolerance is very difficult to diagnose and symptoms like diarrhea, colic and skin rashes can be misdiagnosed as a food allergy.

If there is no history of allergy in the family and your child has a mild reaction to a particular food, it doesn't mean that you should never give that food to your child again. By regularly eating small portions of that food your baby may in time build up antibodies. Many children outgrow early allergies to food by the age of three, and there is no evidence that delaying the introduction of foods such as eggs or wheat until after six months will prevent allergy, except in high-risk babies.

High-risk babies are those with a family history of what is called **atopic** disease – hay fever, asthma, eczema and so on. In this case there are almost certainly advantages in breast-feeding for at least four to six months and in not introducing foods such as cow's milk, eggs and wheat-based products until after six months, by which time the baby's own immune system has had time to mature.

Breast milk is the best choice for babies who are sensitive to cow's milk. However, the breast-feeding mother may need to limit the amount of dairy products she eats herself or she may inadvertently pass them through her milk to her baby.

There has been a trend for parents to give soy milks in the hope of preventing allergic disease or if they believe their baby is showing allergic symptoms. I think that there is little point in doing this. Soy milk does not prevent the development of allergy, even in high-risk babies, nor is it a particularly effective treatment for most forms of milk allergy. Almost as many babies are allergic to soy milks as are allergic to cow's milk, and soy milk inhibits the absorption of certain key minerals including iron.

Ideally, high-risk babies should be breast-fed for at least six months when possible.

My advice is that if you suspect that your baby is allergic, don't be in a hurry to take foods out of her diet. Try the food on several occasions. If you are getting the same symptoms each time then you should seek medical advice, especially if you are removing an important food such as milk or wheat. It may be better in the long run to accept minor symptoms rather than make a major decision that might result in nutritional deficiencies.

The most common foods that can sometimes carry a risk of allergic reactions are cow's milk and dairy products, eggs, fish (especially shellfish) and nuts. Other possible problem foods are wheat and citrus fruits. Artificial colorings and food additives can also induce allergic reactions. If a child is allergic to commonly eaten foods, then a special diet may be necessary.

Much has been made of withholding gluten (wheat-based products) until six months. However, there is no scientific proof that withholding gluten after the age of four months reduces the chances of developing an allergy. However, if there is a family history of gluten intolerance, then you should definitely seek medical advice as gluten sensitivity can induce celiac disease which, although rare, can be very serious. Gluten is found in wheat, rye, barley and oats. Since flour and bread are such staple elements in our diet, the exclusion of gluten would mean a considerable change in diet. However, corn flour, potato flour, tapioca, rice and buckwheat pasta are all safe for your baby to eat.

THE MILLION-DOLLAR SMILE

Cutting teeth can be a painful business, but I often wonder whether teething is worse for the baby or the parents who are kept up all night. When the teeth do arrive, parents coax their children into regular brushing, only to find that around the age of seven, these prized white pearls become the property of the tooth fairy!

Visiting the dentist should hold no fears for a child with healthy teeth and he should love brandishing his "Mickey Mouse" toothbrush and "I've been to the dentist" smiling crocodile sticker, looking forward to his next visit. If we encourage good dental hygiene and control our child's diet successfully, establishing good eating habits early on, then there is no reason why a child should ever have any tooth decay.

Cultivating a sweet tooth is easy but taming one is a Leviathan task. Bad habits start early. Although a drink with a meal won't do much harm, sometimes toddlers are given sweetened drinks in a bottle or a sipper cup to carry around and it goes into their mouth dozens of times a day. Leaving your baby to suck on a bottle of fruit juice at nap time or bedtime is asking for trouble. Not only is there the risk of choking, but at night there's little saliva in the mouth to wash the acid in the juice away and your baby could develop "baby-bottle mouth syndrome," which occurs when the upper front teeth are decayed by the liquid that bathes them while your child is sleeping. When putting your young child to bed, use only water in the bottle. Even milk contains lactose, which is a form of sugar. As soon as your child is ready, wean him off bottles altogether.

Encourage your child to enjoy eating a wide variety of fruit instead of sugary desserts. It is worth taking a little time to present the fruit attractively to entice him. Calcium-rich foods like cheese, yogurt, milk and nuts are important for strong, healthy teeth. Do not bribe your child with the promise of sweets or ice cream if he is good, and similarly do not offer him a sugary treat if he finishes all his spinach. How about giving **good** food as treats?

About one third of the children in this country will have had cavities in their teeth before the age of five. It is the *frequency* with which children consume sugary foods that does the most damage. A chocolate bar eaten in one go is much better than a package of candies sucked one at a time for hours on end. If you want to give your little one sweet treats, then give them at mealtimes when there is plenty of saliva in the mouth to help "wash" the teeth clean. Young children need to eat snacks; they cannot always eat enough food at mealtimes to get all the nutrients and energy they need. Use your imagination and offer your child raw vegetables with a tasty dip or cheese with fruit (see the chapter Scrumptious Snacks on pages 123 to 131).

Probably 50 percent of our sugar intake is in the form of "hidden sugars" in manufactured foods and drinks like ketchup, breakfast cereals, raisins or soft drinks – a can of spaghetti in tomato sauce contains 3 teaspoons of sugar.

Many people believe that young children are bound to have some fillings, yet with a combination of careful plaque removal and a reduction in the amount and fre-quency of sugar at and between meals, decay can be prevented completely. Nearly all foods contain sugar in one form or another, and every time sugar meets plaque on teeth, acid is produced.

You should start brushing your child's teeth as soon as the first tooth is through. With careful brushing at least twice a day you can dislodge the bacteria that reacts with the sugar to cause decalcification so that decay cannot take place. Children don't have the fine motor control needed to clean their teeth properly until they are about five. Avoid spreading your child's toothbrush with a great dollop of toothpaste; a small pea-sized ball at the end of the brush is quite sufficient.

Fluoride helps to strengthen tooth enamel and is one of the most effective elements in preventing tooth decay. There are many ways in which you can ensure that your child gets adequate fluoride protection, like drinking tap water, brushing with fluoride toothpaste or taking fluoride tablets or drops. Too much fluoride, however, can cause discoloration of the teeth so it is best to consult your dentist before giving fluoride supplements.

BABIES

INTRODUCING SOLIDS

WHEN TO WEAN

For all babies, solids should not be introduced before the age of four months because the protective factors and immune system that help prevent allergy are not yet sufficiently developed. In high-risk infants, allergic reactions to food are less likely with later introduction of solids at six months. However, leaving the introduction of solids much later than six months is not a good idea as babies should start to get used to swallowing food, which, unlike sucking, is not a natural reflex; they should be starting to explore new tastes and textures. After all, a world without food would be a pretty dull place!

Your baby will probably let you know when she is ready to start solids – she may still be hungry after an 8 oz-bottle or need more frequent breast-feedings, she may become more unsettled at night or the interval between feedings may become shorter and shorter. A good indication that she's ready for solids is when your baby starts showing a great interest in your food as you eat. She may even try and grab it!

The first solids are introduced to get your baby used to different flavors and textures. The amount of food eaten to begin with will probably be so small that it will make only a small contribution to your baby's diet. However, introducing healthy foods early on will hopefully lead to healthy eating habits later.

MILK IS MAJOR

Milk is the most important food for the whole first year of life. It provides a large proportion of all nutrients and energy (calories). Therefore, the main drink for a baby should be breast milk or a specially adapted infant formula. Unmodified cow's milk is unsuitable for babies under six months as it is too high in salt and protein, and it is best to continue with breast or formula milk for the first year as it is enriched with vitamins and minerals. It is

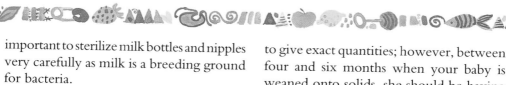

important to sterilize milk bottles and nipples very carefully as milk is a breeding ground for bacteria.

At six months when babies are eating several solid meals a day, they will still need at least 1 pint of breast milk or formula milk. A baby will be getting all the protein she needs from this milk. From six months, ordinary cow's milk and its products – yogurt, cheese and crème fraîche are very useful weaning foods. However, be warned; lurking in a container of fruit yogurt can be up to 6 teaspoons of sugar. It is best to buy natural yogurt or crème fraîche and sweeten it with fruit purée.

Although many of us tend to choose low-fat foods these days, young children need more calories than adults since they grow very rapidly and are physically active. They also have relatively small appetites, so they really need the calorie content of whole milk (see also page 11 for more on this).

Follow-up milk formula is designed for babies of six months to a year who may be having difficulties in coping with solid foods. It contains more iron and vitamins, particularly vitamin D. However in general, a follow-up milk offers few additional benefits compared with a standard formula, so if your baby is coping well with solids, a follow-up milk formula isn't necessary.

Every baby is different so it is not possible to give exact quantities; however, between four and six months when your baby is weaned onto solids, she should be having four or five 8 oz-bottles of milk each day. At around six months, babies should have between 1 pint and 1½ pints of milk each day. Breast-feeding mothers should ideally give around five feedings a day, but once the baby is eating more solids, four should be sufficient. About 15 fl oz a day is recommended for toddlers up to the age of two and of course you can cunningly disguise this in the form of yogurt, scrambled eggs, cream soups or even ice cream.

At around eight to ten months when your baby is able to hold objects in her hands quite well, start to give her milk in a cup (the double-handled plastic cups with weighted bases are good). Inevitably less milk will end up inside your baby and she will become more hungry for solids.

Other Drinks

If your baby is thirsty between milk feedings then offer cooled boiled water rather than sugary drinks.

For older children, too, offer water or some freshly squeezed orange juice. If you do buy cartons of juice, make sure they contain no added sugar. A large cola can contain 10 teaspoons of sugar and many fruit juice drinks contain less than 10 percent juice. These drinks will fill up your child's tummy and take away his appetite. Even pure fruit juices can be extremely sweet and contain fructose, which is bad for teeth, so it's best to dilute them with water before giving them to your child.

FIRST FOODS

Babies are born with a natural sweet tooth; after all breast milk is sweet, so I prefer to introduce savory foods first and then move on to fruits. On pages 27 to 28 is a list of vegetables and fruits for very young babies and how to prepare them.

Packaged baby rice is a good first food; it is bland and easily digested and combines well with fruit and vegetable purées, water or milk. Choose one that is fortified with vitamins and minerals and be careful to check the list of ingredients to make sure there is no added sugar.

Salt should not be added to your baby's food before one year because a baby's kidneys are not mature enough to cope with it. Try using herbs instead of salt to add flavor.

To begin with give your baby single-ingredient purées, starting with foods that have a fairly mild taste (vegetables with a slightly sweet flavor like carrots or squash are popular). Once your baby gets used to the taste of a variety of individual foods, you can begin combining foods. (See page 31 and recipes on pages 34 to 42 in the chapter 6 to 9 Months.) Remember that steaming or microwaving preserves more nutrients than simmering in water.

A lot of people advise giving the same purée for three to four days and then going on to another one once you are sure there is no adverse reaction. In my experience, if you are looking for symptoms then you are almost bound to find them. There is the danger that parents will remove foods from their baby's diet unnecessarily. Unless there is a history of allergy in the family, there is no reason why your baby shouldn't eat a variety of foods each day.

At the beginning, don't expect your baby to take more than 1-2 teaspoons of solids.

A FEW TIPS BEFORE YOU START

◆   For the first few weeks of weaning put most foods through a food mill, blender or food processor to make sure they are really smooth; make them quite runny so that they are easy for your baby to swallow.

◆   Hygiene is paramount when it comes to preparing baby food and feeding your baby. Always wash your hands first. Make sure all the utensils are thoroughly cleaned and sterilize the spoons that go into your baby's mouth.

◆ Don't give your baby new foods at bedtime or you may be kept up all night coping with gas!

◆ Sometimes it is a good idea to give your baby a little milk before his solids so that he is not frantically hungry – you may find this will encourage him to be more receptive to new tastes.

◆ Buy some special weaning spoons, which are shallow and make it easier for your baby to take the food with his lips. Don't be in a hurry to take the spoon out of your baby's mouth as it may take him a while to lick the food off the spoon. Never try to force your baby to eat.

◆ If your baby is not keen on certain foods, try mixing them with familiar tastes like breast or formula milk or baby rice.

◆ Don't be put off if your baby spits the food out. A natural reaction when a baby sucks is to push his tongue forward, so often the food you put in comes straight out again. Don't be discouraged because it doesn't mean he dislikes the taste. Swallowing is a skill your baby will need to learn so be patient. Smile and encourage your baby; after all eating should be fun.

◆ Don't spoon food out of a bowl into your baby's mouth and then refrigerate the remainder for the next day. Food in the bowl could become contaminated by bacteria from your baby's mouth.

◆ Make eating fun: if possible sit opposite your baby and smile and encourage her. Let her see you eating; babies are great mimics and if they see you enjoying food . . .

EQUIPMENT

You don't need to rush out and buy loads of special equipment to make your own baby food. However, it is worth investing in the following items.

◆ *FOOD MILL:* This is a hand-turned device that is not expensive to buy and that gets rid of all the indigestible bits like the skins of vegetables, the skins of dried fruit, and the seeds of tomatoes, and can be used to make super smooth purées for your baby. It is especially useful when preparing small quantities.

◆ *BLENDER OR FOOD PROCESSOR*: Some food processors have mini attachments for making small quantities – this is particularly useful for making baby purées. Electric hand blenders are also good for making foods like apples or carrots into smooth purées. Foods with tough skins or seeds are better puréed in a food mill.

◆ *STEAMER*: Steaming foods helps to preserve nutrients and the food tastes much better as none of the flavor is lost in the cooking liquid. A multilayered steamer is good for cooking several foods at once. I think that once you have tasted steamed vegetables, you will want to cook them that way for the whole family.

PREPARING AHEAD AND FREEZING

Who has time to fool around in the kitchen with young babies in the house, you may well ask? Homemade purées should be eaten either on the day they are prepared or refrigerated and eaten the next day, but this is where a freezer becomes invaluable. In a couple of hours I can prepare a whole month's food supply for my baby. I nearly always prepare recipes in bulk and that way I have a constant supply of homemade convenience foods.

It's so simple to freeze food in ice cube trays or little containers and, once frozen, transfer them to freezer bags. Nearly all the recipes in this book are suitable for freezing (those not suitable are marked ❄). Cooked purées should last for between four and six months in a good freezer. Always label the food with the expiration date to make sure you never give food to your baby that is past its prime.

◆   Freeze food as soon as you can after it has been cooked. However, do not put warm food into the freezer; it makes your freezer work too hard and causes ice crystals to form.

◆   Freezing can dry out purées so you may have to add some liquid like milk, stock or juice when you reheat them.

◆   If you have friends with babies roughly the same age you could each prepare two or three recipes in bulk and then swap half of your food for half of your friend's recipes, thereby spending only half as long in the kitchen.

◆   Always reheat food thoroughly so that it is piping hot. Microwaves are great for cooking frozen food but make sure you stir the food to get an even distribution of heat. Let the food cool down a little and test the temperature of the food yourself before giving it to your baby.

◆   Apart from banana, avocado, melon and eggplant, most fruit and vegetable purées freeze very well.

4 TO 6 MONTHS

FIRST FRUITS

APPLE AND PEAR   Peel, core and cut into pieces. Simmer in enough water to cover or steam until soft (pears will cook more quickly). To microwave, chop the peeled apple or pear, sprinkle with a little water or pure apple juice, cover and cook on full power for 1½ to 3 minutes until soft. Purée in a blender.

BANANA AND PAPAYA   These need no cooking. Peel the fruit and purée in a blender or, for older babies, mash with a fork. Add a little boiled water, pure fruit juice or breast or formula milk if the banana is too thick and sticky for your baby to swallow. Another method is to bake the banana in its skin in the oven (at 350°F) until the skin turns black, then peel and mash the banana – this brings out the sweetness in the fruit and makes it nice and soft. Be warned, however, that some babies find banana difficult to digest.

FIRST VEGETABLES

CARROTS OR ZUCCHINI   Baby carrots are very sweet so you could try using these sometimes. Peel, trim and slice the carrots, either steam until tender or simmer in water. Purée in a blender. If the carrots are steamed you will need to add some of the water from the steamer to make a smooth purée. It is best to steam zucchini and, since they naturally contain a lot of water, you probably won't need to add any.

To microwave zucchini or carrots, trim the ends, cut into slices, sprinkle with water, and cover. Zucchini will take about 3 minutes on full power and carrots about 5 minutes.

POTATOES, RUTABAGA, PARSNIP OR SWEET POTATO   Rutabaga, parsnip and sweet potato have an appealingly sweet taste that babies love. Peel the vegetables and cut into chunks. Cover with water, bring to a boil and simmer until tender. Alternatively, you could bake the potato or sweet potato in the oven at 350°F for about 1 hour (or until soft). Prick the skin and place on a foil-lined pan, turning after 30 minutes.

Small quantities are more economically cooked in a microwave. Prick the skin of the potato, put into a shallow microwave-proof dish and microwave on full power for 7 to 9 minutes or until tender. To microwave parsnip or rutabaga, cook with water, covered, for about 5 minutes on full power. Purée in a blender, adding some of the cooking water or breast or formula milk to make a smooth purée.

BUTTERNUT OR ACORN SQUASH OR PUMPKIN   There are several ways of cooking squash or pumpkin, but baking in the oven caramelizes their natural sugars and gives them the best flavor. Cut the squash in half, scoop out the seeds and brush the flesh generously with melted butter. Place on foil and bake in an oven preheated to 350°F for 40 minutes or until tender. If the flesh starts to dry out, cover with foil. Alternatively, proceed as above, place in a microwave-proof dish and cook on full power for between 10 and 12 minutes or until soft. You could also cut squash or pumpkin into chunks, simmer in water or sauté in butter until tender.

CREAM OF FRUIT OR VEGETABLE PURÉE   Mixing fruit or vegetable purées with baby rice and milk is often a good way of introducing new foods, particularly foods with a strong taste like broccoli.

cream of pumpkin

Pumpkin is a much-neglected vegetable, but I find that babies love the flavor. You could use rutabaga here if you prefer.

1 cup chopped pumpkin
Knob of butter or margarine
1 tablespoon baby rice
3 tablespoons formula milk

For the best flavor I cook the pumpkin in the oven until tender (about 40 minutes at 350°F) with a little butter or margarine. Alternatively, you can sauté it in a pan until tender or simmer it in water or stock, or cook it in the microwave on full power for 10 to 12 minutes.

Purée the cooked pumpkin or roughly chop. Mix the baby rice with the milk and stir into the pumpkin.

Makes 2 portions

6 TO 9 MONTHS

There will be a lot of change in your baby's life between six and nine months. She will start sitting up and will be able to sit in a high chair, and she will spend many more hours awake. She will probably have cut a few teeth and she will begin to feed herself although her aim will be far from perfect. Your baby will be starting to learn to chew so you can vary the texture of her food a little more – mashing, mincing or chopping. Babies at this stage can eat between 1 and 4 tablespoons of food three times a day.

You may need to limit foods your child might find indigestible like spinach, dried fruit, lentils, citrus and berry fruits. You can now buy lots of unusual fruits and vegetables in supermarkets like sharon fruit, a variety of persimmon from Israel, or acorn squash. Many of these are simple to prepare and although they may seem a little more expensive than ordinary fruits and vegetables, you can make a lot of portions from them and they are great mixed with other foods, e.g., sharon fruit and crème fraîche or acorn squash and apple. Although your baby will still be breast-fed or drinking formula milk, cow's milk is fine for mixing in foods and for cooking.

At around six months, chicken, fish and meat can be introduced. Chicken combines well with lots of different foods and chicken stock forms the basis of many of my recipes. Fish is good too – quick to cook and nice and soft – but take special care to check that *all* bones have been removed. Choose flounder or hake (a type of cod) to begin with as they have the smoothest texture. Liver is probably the best meat to start with as it is very nutritious and, again, purées to a very smooth consistency.

MORE FRUITS

Remember that raw is best so try giving your baby mashed or grated fruits as soon as you think she can cope with them.

PEACHES, PLUMS AND APRICOTS To skin these fruits easily, cut a shallow cross in the skin, submerge in boiling water for 1 minute and then plunge in cold water and peel. Cut the fruit into pieces and discard the pit. Simmer in enough water to cover until soft, or steam. To microwave, add a little water, cover and microwave on full power for 2 to 3 minutes until soft. Then purée.

MELON Cantaloupe is a rich source of vitamin C and A, and a good ripe honeydew melon has a sweet taste that babies love. Cut the melon in half, scoop out the seeds, cut the flesh into chunks and mash or purée. Do not freeze.

DRIED FRUIT Dried fruit tends to have a laxative effect on young babies and prunes are good if your baby is constipated. For young babies it is a good idea to mix dried fruit purées with milk and baby rice, yogurt or crème fraîche. If the dried fruit is very hard then soak in hot water for a couple of hours before cooking. Cover the fruit with water and simmer until soft (about 10 minutes). Purée in a food mill to get rid of the tough skins.

BERRY FRUITS These can be quite indigestible for babies so give them in moderation or mixed with other fruits, e.g., banana or apple. Steam, simmer in a little water or microwave covered for about 1 minute on full power. Purée in a food mill to get rid of the seeds. Cooked berry fruits tend to be quite watery so try mixing in some baby rice to thicken the purée.

MORE VEGETABLES

BROCCOLI AND CAULIFLOWER Wash the vegetables carefully and cut into small florets. Steam until tender and purée in a blender or food mill with some of the steaming water or milk. Alternatively, simmer in water. To cook in a microwave, sprinkle with water, cover and cook for 3 minutes on full power or until tender.

GREEN BEANS Remove stems, tips and any strings. If using long runner beans then cut them diagonally into about 3 pieces. Steam until tender. Alternatively microwave on full power, covered, for about 3 minutes. Runner beans are best puréed in a food mill for young babies to get rid of the indigestible parts. Add a little boiled water or milk to make a smooth purée.

SPINACH Wash the spinach leaves carefully, removing the coarse stalks, and steam until tender. Alternatively, put the leaves into a pan with just a little water (or use frozen spinach to save time). Simmer, covered, until tender. Purée in a food mill or blender. For microwave cooking, sprinkle

with water and cook on full power for about 4 minutes.

FRESH PEAS Steam until tender or cover fresh, shelled peas or frozen peas with water and simmer until tender. Purée in a food mill to get rid of the skins and add a little of the cooking liquid or some milk to make a smooth consistency. To microwave, add a little water and cook, covered, for 3 to 4 minutes or until soft. (Frozen peas will need less time.)

BELL PEPPERS To skin peppers, cut them in half, remove the white core and seeds, flatten them with your hand and rub the skin with oil. Place under a preheated broiler until the skin has blackened. Let cool and the skin will rub off easily. Purée with milk or cooled boiled water.

WINNING COMBINATIONS

Once your baby has been introduced to a fairly wide range of single-ingredient purées then you can start mixing foods together – below are some combinations that I have found babies like and I hope this list will give you inspiration to try some ideas of your own. A good test, of course, is to taste them yourself because if you think they're delicious, chances are that baby will agree! Don't be afraid to mix unusual combina-

tions. Adding fruit to foods that your child refuses to eat often encourages her to eat. When Lara was two, she flatly refused to eat chicken and no amount of cajoling or bribery would make her change her mind. I made up a recipe combining apples (one of her favorites) and the dreaded chicken and she kept on asking for more until there was none left. In my experience the more you want children to eat something, the less likely they are to oblige you, so I find that this gradual introduction makes a great compromise.

APPLES OR PEARS AND . . .

cinnamon

vanilla extract

dried fruit, e.g., raisins, prunes, apricots and custard

yogurt, crème fraîche or sieved cottage cheese
blackberries
cereals, e.g., baby rice, oats
chicken
cottage cheese or cream cheese
butternut squash
carrots
sweet potato
blueberries
raisins and crème fraîche
pumpkin or squash
plums
prunes

BANANAS AND . . .

yogurt or crème fraîche
avocado
zucchini
dried fruit
kiwi
strawberries and crème fraîche or yogurt
raspberries
chicken
yogurt and honey
tangerines
papaya

SQUASH AND . . .

apples
pears
peaches
grapes
cinnamon
spinach
chicken
carrot and crème fraîche

PASTA AND . . .

spinach and cheese
apples and carrots
zucchini, tomato and onions
tomato and cheese
ground meat, eggplant and tomatoes
liver, onion and mushrooms
chicken, leeks and cream
cheese sauce and vegetables

CHICKEN AND . . .

grapes with cream sauce
apple
rice and tomatoes
cottage cheese and pineapple or peach
avocado
green beans and apple juice
peaches and rice
potato and tomato
pumpkin and grapes

BEEF AND . . .

pasta, tomatoes and onions
carrots, potatoes and onions
liver, eggplant and tomatoes
barley and prunes
rice and mushrooms

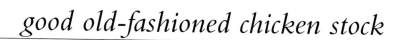

good old-fashioned chicken stock

Chicken stock forms the basis of so many of my recipes. It's very simple to make and full of goodness for your baby. I prepare it in bulk (usually cooking two chickens) and then freeze it in 2-cup portions. For maximum flavor I make the stock from a stewing chicken with its giblets. Otherwise a good stock can be made using the carcass from a roast chicken with as many giblets as possible. If your butcher has any veal bones available these can also be used to enhance the flavor of the stock.

1 large stewing chicken plus giblets
8 cups water
2 large onions, peeled and roughly chopped
3 large carrots, scrubbed and roughly sliced
2 parsnips, scrubbed and roughly chopped

1 small turnip, washed and cut into chunks
2 leeks, white part only, sliced
Half a celery stalk and a handful of celery leaves
2 sprigs of parsley
1 bay leaf
2 or 3 chicken stock cubes (optional for babies over one year)

Wash the chicken and giblets, trimming away excess fat. Alternatively break up the carcass of the roast chicken. Put into a large pan and cover with water. Bring to a boil slowly and remove the scum from the surface. Add all the remaining ingredients and simmer very gently for about 3½ – 4 hours. Remove the chicken when it is tender (after about 2 hours), strip off all the meat (to use in other dishes) and then return the carcass to the pan.

Refrigerate overnight and in the morning you can remove the layer of fat that settles on top. Simply strain for a lovely rich stock. This also makes a wonderful clear soup with some vermicelli or bow-tie pasta.

makes about 6 cups

vegetable stock

For young babies leave out the peppercorns but for older babies they will improve the flavor.

1 lb carrots	*1-2 tablespoons butter or margarine*
1 lb onions	*1 bouquet garni*
Top half of a celery stalk	*A few black peppercorns*
1 small parsnip	*12 cups water*
½ small turnip	

Peel and wash the vegetables. Dry them and slice them into big pieces and then sauté in butter or margarine over low heat until lightly browned. Add the rest of the ingredients, pour in the water and bring to a boil. Cover and simmer for about 3 hours. Strain, allow to cool and refrigerate for several hours. Remove any fat from the top and freeze the stock in 2-cup containers.

makes about 8 cups

baby muesli

Combining oat flakes with milk and fruit makes a tasty nutritious breakfast for your baby. For my basic recipe I have used dried apricots and fresh pear. Other good combinations are peach, pear and banana or blueberries, grated apple and apple juice. You can experiment, making your own mueslis with fresh fruit that is in season. This is good for older children, too, served hot on a cold winter's morning.

6 dried apricots
⅔ cup milk
⅓ oat flakes

1 large or 2 small pears, peeled, cored
and cut into pieces

Simmer the apricots in water until soft (about 10 minutes). Meanwhile, heat the milk in a saucepan, stir in the oats, bring to a boil and simmer, stirring occasionally, for 3 to 4 minutes. Once cooked, set aside. Add the pears to the apricots, adding a little more water if necessary and simmer for about 3 minutes. Blend the fruit together with the oats. For young babies put through a food mill to make into a smooth purée.

makes 4 portions

fruit purée flavored with vanilla

Simmering fruit with a vanilla bean is a good way of adding extra sweetness without added sugar. I've added kiwi because it is a good source of vitamin C but you need a sweet one. Otherwise, use peach or pear.

1 apple, peeled, cored and sliced
2 plums, peeled and cut into pieces
1 small piece of vanilla bean or a drop
of pure vanilla extract
1 kiwi fruit, peeled and sliced

Simmer the apple and plum in a little water, together with the vanilla bean, until soft. Remove the vanilla bean and purée together with the sliced kiwi. Push through a sieve for young babies to get rid of the little black seeds.

makes 3 portions

Cinderella's pumpkin

This is one of Scarlett's favorite combinations — and it tastes so good you could make it as a soup for the rest of the family. If you can't find pumpkin, try butternut squash instead.

1½ cups peeled, cubed pumpkin
⅓ cup sliced leek, white part only
Knob of butter

¼ cup chicken or vegetable stock (see pages 33–34)

Put the pumpkin into a saucepan, cover with water and simmer until soft. Meanwhile, sauté the leek in butter until soft. Combine the cooked pumpkin and leek, pour over the stock and simmer for 2 to 3 minutes. Mash with a fork or purée.

makes 3–4 portions

butternut squash

Butternut squash is pear-shaped, beige on the outside and orange inside; it's not expensive and can be found in large supermarkets. It combines well with lots of different fruits and vegetables and this combination is a winner with my baby daughter when peaches are in season. See Winning Combinations (pages 31–32) for other ideas.

1 small butternut or acorn squash
1-2 tablespoons butter or margarine, melted

¼ teaspoon cinnamon (optional)
2 peaches, peeled
Milk, stock or water to purée

Preheat the oven to 350°F .
Cut the squash in half, scoop out the seeds, brush with melted butter or margarine and sprinkle with cinnamon, if using. Bake it until soft (about 50 minutes). Meanwhile steam the peaches for about 6 minutes. Combine the peaches with the squash and add as much milk, stock or water as necessary to make a smooth purée.

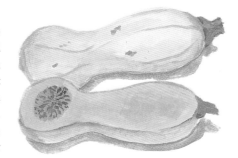

makes 8 portions

broccoli trio

Potato makes a great thickener for any vegetable purée so you can experiment with new combinations using it as a base. Another good thickener is sieved hard-boiled egg yolks – they also provide a good source of iron.

*1 large potato, peeled
and chopped
½ cup broccoli florets*

*1 medium zucchini, sliced
1–2 tablespoons milk*

Steam the potato (in the bottom of a steamer, if you have one) for about 12 minutes and steam the other vegetables for 8 to 10 minutes. Simply blend all the ingredients to the required purée.

makes 4 portions

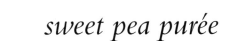

sweet pea purée

The sautéed onions and peas give this purée a naturally sweet taste that
appeals to babies.

1 tablespoon chopped onion
1 tablespoon butter or margarine
1 small zucchini, sliced

⅓ cup frozen peas
½ cup chicken or vegetable stock (see
pages 33–34)

Sauté the onion in the butter or margarine until soft, add the zucchini and
sauté for 2 minutes, then add the peas and the stock. Simmer for about 4
minutes or until tender. Purée in a blender or food mill.

makes 3 portions

green-eyed monster

I call this the green-eyed monster as all the ingredients are green and the green eyes
are the pods inside the beans. French beans are best because the pods are
tiny. If you use runner beans purée through a food mill for young babies.

1 cup green beans, stems and tips
removed

1 medium zucchini, sliced
2 tablespoons apple juice

Steam beans and zucchini until tender, about 6 minutes. Mix with the apple juice
and purée.

makes 4 portions

chicken with winter vegetables

This makes a lovely smooth-textured purée.

½ cup chicken, cut into pieces
½ tablespoon chopped onion
2 tablespoons chopped celery
2 tablespoons chopped leek
1 medium carrot, scrubbed and sliced
½ cup peeled and chopped rutabaga

1 medium potato, peeled and cut into
cubes
1¼ cups water
2 tablespoons yogurt or
crème fraîche

Put the chicken and the vegetables into a saucepan and cover with the water. Simmer covered for about 20 minutes or until the vegetables are soft. Purée with some of the cooking liquid and the yogurt or crème fraîche.

makes 6 portions

creamy pink purée

A good way to turn some leftover cooked chicken into a tasty meal for your baby. This is especially good if you add a slice of avocado.

¼ cup cooked, chopped chicken
¼ cup milk

1 tomato, peeled, seeded and cut into
pieces

Simply blend all the ingredients together to a purée.

makes 2 portions

one-pot chicken with garden vegetables

My daughter Scarlett loved this when she first started to eat chicken and
it's very simple to make.

⅓ cup rice
1¼ cups chicken or vegetable stock (see
pages 33–34)
1 small chicken breast, cut into pieces

¼ cup broccoli florets
1 small carrot, scrubbed and sliced
¼ cup chopped green beans
½ cup apple juice

Cook the rice in the stock. When
the rice is half-cooked, add the
chicken, vegetables and the apple
juice. Continue to cook until the rice
is soft and the vegetables tender, but
not overcooked. If necessary, add
extra stock to make the purée a good
consistency.

makes 4 portions

liver and apple purée

Liver blends to a lovely smooth consistency; it's very nutritious and cheap
to buy; and combining it with apple will appeal to your baby.

¼ lb lamb's or calf's liver
¼ cup milk

1 apple, peeled, cored and cut into
pieces

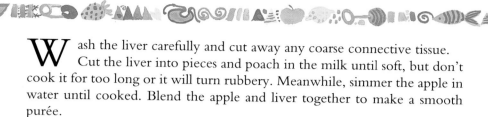

W ash the liver carefully and cut away any coarse connective tissue. Cut the liver into pieces and poach in the milk until soft, but don't cook it for too long or it will turn rubbery. Meanwhile, simmer the apple in water until cooked. Blend the apple and liver together to make a smooth purée.

makes 3 portions

beginner's beef casserole

The carrot and rutabaga add a sweetness that babies like. This is an ideal recipe for introducing red meat and it can be puréed to a smooth consistency. This recipe takes a while to cook but it's not labor-intensive.

1 small onion, peeled and sliced
½ small clove garlic, finely chopped (optional)
Margarine or vegetable oil for sautéing
⅓ lb lean stewing beef, cut into cubes
1 medium carrot, scrubbed and sliced

1 sprig of parsley
1¼ cups beef, chicken or vegetable stock (see pages 33–34)
1 medium potato, peeled and cut into cubes
¾ cup peeled, cubed rutabaga

P reheat the oven to 350°F. Sauté the onion and garlic in the margarine or oil until soft, then add the meat and brown. Put into a small casserole with the carrot and parsley and add half the stock. Put in the oven and after 10 minutes turn the temperature down to 325°F. After 1 hour, add the potato and rutabaga and pour in the rest of the stock; continue to cook for another hour. Blend to the desired consistency.

makes 5 portions

melt-in-the-mouth fish with mushrooms

A great way of adding taste is to flavor the milk in which you cook the fish – in this recipe I have used mace, onion, peppercorns and a bay leaf. You can substitute four peeled, halved, seedless grapes for the button mushrooms as a delicious variation.

A pinch of mace
2 peppercorns
1 slice of onion
½ bay leaf
⅔ cup milk
2 tablespoons finely chopped onion

1-2 tablespoons butter or margarine
2 button mushrooms, chopped
1 tablespoon flour
¼ lb skinless fillet of flounder or sole
Knob of butter
Small pinch mixed herbs

Add the mace, peppercorns, onion and bay leaf to the milk and heat without boiling for about 5 minutes. Meanwhile sauté the onion in the butter until soft and then add the chopped mushrooms; cook for a couple of minutes. Stir in the flour, let it cook for a minute and then gradually add the strained milk to make a thick white sauce. Steam or microwave the fish with a little milk, butter or margarine and herbs for 3–4 minutes, or until the fish flakes easily with a fork (check carefully for any bones). Mix with the sauce and purée in a blender.

makes 2 portions

9 TO 12 MONTHS

It is easy to continue making smooth purées and underestimate your baby's ability to chew. However, once your baby has cut a few teeth, vary the texture of the food; try mashing, chopping and grating food – you may be surprised by what a few teeth and strong gums can get through!

At this age, babies are often more interested in the feel than the taste of their food so it is a good idea to have two bowls, one for baby and one for you. That way you can sneak spoonfuls into her mouth while she's busy moisturizing her hair with spinach purée! It is also helpful to give your baby lots of soft finger foods. Put a waterproof tablecloth under the high chair (this way you can recycle foods that have mysteriously disappeared) and scatter lots of soft, colorful finger foods on the high chair tray. Your baby will really enjoy picking up all the different foods and popping them in her mouth, and this will also improve her hand and eye coordination.

Once your baby is able to hold toys fairly well, try a cup with a spout. When your baby can manage that, remove the top. This is the messy bit. A cup with a weighted base that doesn't topple over is the best choice but make sure she isn't wearing her best clothes!

Remember, never leave your child unattended while eating and avoid giving foods that might get stuck in her throat like whole grapes, fruits with pits or nuts. Peanuts are especially dangerous because they are just the right size to block the esophagus.

IDEAS FOR FINGER FOODS

◆ *steamed vegetables, e.g., potato, zucchini, cauliflower or broccoli*
◆ *dried fruits*
◆ *grated apple, pear, cucumber or carrot*
◆ *fresh fruits, e.g., chunks of banana, or orange segments*
◆ *cooked peas or sweet corn*
◆ *breakfast cereals like corn flakes mixed with a little milk*
◆ *grated cheese*

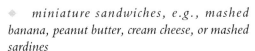

◆ *miniature sandwiches, e.g., mashed banana, peanut butter, cream cheese, or mashed sardines*

◆ *cooked pasta shapes like little bow-ties or shells*

◆ *little pieces of cooked chicken or flaked fish*

◆ *miniature meat or chicken balls*

◆ *fingers of toast to dip into vegetable purées*

◆ *rice cakes*

THE QUESTION OF MILK

As I've already explained, it's best to continue with formula milk or breast milk for the first year because it is enriched with vitamins and minerals. However, the good news is that once your baby gets to around 11 months and is crawling around and sticking everything into his mouth, there is not much point in sterilizing bottles – just make sure they are washed very thoroughly. Be careful not to let milk sit around in bottles and curdle. Wash them as soon after use as possible. If you have a dishwasher, rinse them out very well and then put them in the machine. Your baby should be able to drink from a cup now, so maybe just offer a bottle at bedtime.

THE CEREAL KILLERS

You can now introduce adult breakfast cereals like oatmeal, corn flakes, granola and muesli. There is no need to continue with baby cereals, which are more expensive, fine textured and tend to be quite bland. However, beware! The once healthy bowl of cereal is looking more and more like a bowl of candy. Look carefully at the labels; some cereals contain as much as 49 percent sugar. Choose whole-grain cereals that are low in sugar and salt.

TEETHING

Chewing on something cold and hard can relieve sore gums. Choose something hard so that your baby can't chew off chunks and choke on them and never leave a baby alone with food.

◆ Trimmed celery stalks.

◆ Chilled scraped carrot.

◆ Cool chunks of cantaloupe or honeydew melon.

◆ The hard core of a pineapple.

◆ Semifrozen banana – as this defrosts it will turn into mush in your baby's mouth.

◆ Dried apple rings – your baby can poke her fingers through the hole to hold onto this; you could secure it to the high chair with a piece of string to stop it from falling on the floor.

◆ A piece of bagel.

◆ A rice cake.

◆ Moisten a clean cloth with cold water, wring it out and let your baby chew on it. When Scarlett was nine months old, she

was always chewing on bits of her clothes so this is a good alternative.

◆ You can buy teething rings filled with liquid, which you can chill in the fridge – don't store a teething ring in the freezer, though, as it will be so cold it could burn your baby's gums.

Rusks

Manufacturers state that adding sugar to baby foods is undesirable but then they add it to baby rusks (zwieback). Some contain more sugar than a doughnut. It's simple to make your own sugar-free baby toast. Simply cut a thick slice of bread into three strips and bake in an oven preheated to 350°F for 15 minutes. You can store these in an airtight container for three or four days. If your child gets frustrated trying to use a spoon, you can also prepare fingers of toast and your baby can have fun dipping these into vegetable purées.

stuffed potato

If you are baking potatoes in the oven then why not add an extra one for your baby and make this delicious recipe? Alternatively, simply boil the potato and then mix in the rest of the ingredients.

1 medium to large potato
1 cup cauliflower or broccoli florets
2 tomatoes, skinned, seeded and chopped

2 tablespoons grated Cheddar cheese
A knob of butter
3–4 tablespoons milk

Preheat the oven to 400°F. Prick the potato and bake it in the oven until soft. Meanwhile, steam the cauliflower or broccoli until tender. Peel the skin off the potato and mix all the ingredients together with the cooked potato. Process in a blender or mash with a fork.

makes 3 portions

"I don't like vegetables" purée

There are two vegetables that are seldom on a list of children's favorites, so as a challenge I decided to combine them; after a bit of experimenting this was the recipe that got the seal of approval.

½ cup Brussels sprouts
½ cup broccoli florets
1 tablespoon butter or margarine
1 tablespoon flour

½ cup milk
A pinch of freshly grated nutmeg
(optional)
⅓ cup grated Cheddar cheese

Steam the vegetables until tender, taking care not to overcook them. Melt the butter or margarine in a saucepan, add the flour and cook, stirring, for 1 minute. Add the milk gradually, stirring until the sauce thickens and boils. Make a cheese sauce in the usual way (see page 47), season with the nutmeg and add the cheese. Pour the sauce over the vegetables and blend or chop for older babies.

makes 3 portions

Popeye purée

Egg yolk and spinach are both rich in iron; you will improve the absorption of the iron in these foods if you give your baby some vitamin C-rich foods at the same meal (e.g., kiwi fruit or orange segments).

8 oz fresh spinach
1-2 tablespoons butter or margarine
1 tablespoon flour
½ cup milk

⅓ cup grated Cheddar cheese
A pinch of freshly grated nutmeg
½ hard-boiled egg, finely grated

Remove any tough stalks from the spinach and wash carefully. Cook it, in a little water, until tender. Meanwhile make a white sauce: melt the butter or margarine in a saucepan, stir in the flour and let it cook for 1 minute. Add the milk gradually, stirring over a gentle heat until the sauce thickens and boils. Stir in the cheese and nutmeg. Squeeze any excess water from the spinach, mix with the sauce and purée or chop. Finally add the grated egg.

makes 4 portions

lettuce, cauliflower and zucchini purée

This purée tastes so good that I always make a large quantity; I freeze some for my baby and serve the rest as soup for everyone else in the family.

1 onion, peeled and chopped
1-2 tablespoons margarine or 1 tablespoon oil
3 zucchini, washed, trimmed and thinly sliced
1 small cauliflower, chopped

1 small head crisp lettuce, washed and shredded
3 cups chicken or vegetable stock (see pages 33–34)
1¼ cup extra stock to make a soup

Sauté the onion in the margarine or oil until soft but not golden. Add the zucchini, cauliflower and lettuce and cook over low heat for about 4 minutes. Add the stock and continue to cook for about 15 minutes over low heat. Remove about a quarter of the liquid and vegetables and purée in a blender to make the baby's portions. Add the extra stock to the rest and blend to make a delicious smooth soup.

makes 6 baby portions and 4 adult portions

minestrone magic

Babies love fishing out the different ingredients in this soup. Older children love it too; "Can you catch a green bean?" asks Lara, and Nicholas fishes deep into his bowl with his soup spoon. This game seems to last a long time and second helpings are usually requested to replenish stocks!

1 large onion, peeled and finely sliced
1 clove garlic, crushed
Oil for sautéing
2 medium carrots, scrubbed and diced
1 celery stalk, diced
2 medium potatoes, peeled and diced
1 can (8 oz) tomatoes, chopped
8 cups chicken or vegetable stock (see pages 33–34)

½ cup shredded cabbage
½ cup sliced green beans
½ cup tiny pasta shapes
⅓ cup frozen peas
1 can (15 oz) navy (pea) beans
Freshly ground black pepper
3 tablespoons freshly grated Parmesan cheese (optional)

Sauté the onion and garlic in the oil until the onions are softened, then add the carrots and celery. Transfer to a large saucepan, add the diced potatoes, tomatoes and their juice and the stock, and simmer for about 20 minutes. Add the cabbage, green beans and pasta and simmer for another 10 minutes. Finally stir in the frozen peas and the navy beans and cook for another 5 minutes. Season with a little freshly ground black pepper and sprinkle with some Parmesan, if you like.

makes 20 portions

mock baked beans

Small white (navy or pea) beans are the beans of "baked beans". They are an excellent source of protein. This is my tasty homemade version of a popular dish.

⅔ cup dried navy (pea) beans or 1
small can (15 oz)
1 medium onion, peeled and chopped
1-2 tablespoons butter or margarine
1½ tablespoons flour
1¼ cups milk

4 medium tomatoes, skinned, seeded
and chopped
1 tablespoon tomato purée
1 bay leaf
½ cup frozen peas

If you're using dried beans, soak them in water overnight or for at least 5 hours. Strain, cover with fresh water, bring to a boil and then simmer for 2 hours, checking from time to time that there is still enough water.

Sauté the onion in the butter or margarine until transparent, then stir in the flour. Cook for a minute before gradually adding the milk. Bring the sauce to a boil, then reduce the heat. Add the chopped tomatoes, tomato purée and the bay leaf and simmer for 10 minutes. Meanwhile cook the peas. Strain the beans once they are cooked (they should be quite soft), remove the bay leaf and mix them together with the tomato sauce and peas. Mash with a fork or purée in a blender or food mill if your baby finds these beans hard to digest.

makes 8 portions

creamy fish with tomatoes

Cooking fish in parchment paper or foil seals in the flavor and saves on clean-up! I use parchment paper when cooking in a microwave and foil when cooking in the oven. Probably the best fish for young babies is flounder or sole because it is very soft and purées well. For older babies who can cope with more lumpy food, then try using haddock or cod. In the following recipe you could use other vegetables like carrots, leeks and zucchini instead of the tomatoes. Try a sprinkling of chopped fresh herbs too.

½ small onion, peeled and chopped
1 tablespoon butter or margarine plus
extra for dotting
2 tomatoes, peeled, seeded and cut into
pieces

1 bay leaf
3 tablespoons crème fraîche or yogurt
¼ cup grated Cheddar cheese (optional)
¼ lb skinned fillet of flounder or sole

S auté the onion in the butter or margarine until soft, then add the tomatoes and bay leaf. Cook them for a couple of minutes and then stir in the crème fraîche or yogurt. Cut the foil or parchment paper into a circle large enough to cover the fish. Place the fish on the foil or paper, dot with a little butter, spoon in the onion and tomato mixture, removing the bay leaf, and sprinkle with cheese. Then fold the circle in half and roll the edges together to form a package.

Cook in a microwave on full power for 3 to 4 minutes or cook in the oven at 350°F, wrapped in foil, for 15 to 20 minutes. Pick out any bones, then purée or chop in a blender, adding a little milk to make into a smooth purée if necessary.

makes 3 portions

fish with broccoli and cheese

This makes a good first fish recipe and it is best to put it through a food mill for young babies. Not only is broccoli a rich source of vitamins A and C, but recent studies show evidence that eating broccoli may help to protect us against certain forms of cancer.

¼-⅓ lb fillet of flounder or sole
1 slice of peeled onion
sprig of parsley or bay leaf
¾ cup milk
½ cup broccoli florets

1 tablespoon butter or margarine
1 tablespoon flour
⅓ cup grated Cheddar or Gruyère cheese

Put the fish fillet into an ovenproof dish, together with the onion and parsley or bay leaf and pour in ¼ cup of the milk. Cover and cook in the oven at 350°F for about 12 minutes or in the microwave on full power for about 3 minutes. The fish will flake easily with a fork when cooked. Meanwhile steam the broccoli for about 5 minutes.

Once the fish is cooked, strain the cooking liquid and flake the fish carefully to make sure there are no bones; set aside. Melt the butter or margarine and stir in the flour. Cook for 30 seconds, then gradually stir in the remaining milk to make a smooth sauce. Stir in the grated cheese and add the cooked broccoli and flaked fish. Blend or put through a food mill to achieve the required consistency.

makes 3 portions

pasta primavera

This is popular with my whole family; you can prepare the sauce in advance and freeze it in small containers to be used at your convenience. If your child is a confirmed non-vegetable eater, resort to disguise and purée the sauce. The type of pasta you use will depend on your baby's eating skills!

2 tablespoons olive oil
1 small onion, peeled and finely chopped
1 small clove garlic, finely choppped
½ red or yellow pepper, seeded and finely chopped
2 medium zucchini, diced
1 cup sliced mushrooms (optional)
2-3 fresh tomatoes skinned, seeded and chopped or 1 can (28 oz)

1 can (28 oz) tomatoes, chopped and drained
1 tablespoon tomato purée
1 tablespoon milk
A little dried basil or oregano (optional)
4 oz pasta
A little grated Parmesan cheese (optional)

Sauté the onion and garlic in the olive oil for about 4 minutes, then add the chopped pepper and continue to cook for 3 to 4 minutes. Add the remaining ingredients, except the pasta and Parmesan, and simmer for about 15 minutes. Meanwhile, cook the pasta in boiling water until tender. Drain the pasta and mix with the sauce when it is ready. Sprinkle with Parmesan if you wish.

makes 5 portions

Lara's tomato and cheese pasta sauce

If your baby or toddler is a pasta groupie, like my daughter Lara, then this sauce is a great way to make sure she's getting a good supply of calcium – so important for healthy bones and teeth. Serve with freshly cooked pasta.

1 large onion, peeled and finely sliced
2 tablespoons vegetable oil
1 can (14 oz) tomatoes, chopped
1 tablespoon tomato purée
½ teaspoon mixed Italian herbs
½ teaspoon oregano

Freshly ground black pepper
¾ cup grated Cheddar or Gruyère cheese
¾ cup grated Mozzarella cheese

Gently sauté the onions in the oil in a covered pan, stirring occasionally, for 15 to 20 minutes until softened but not browned. This will give them a delicious, slightly sweet taste. Stir in the tomatoes, tomato purée, herbs and pepper and simmer for about 10 minutes. Remove from the heat and mix in the cheese until melted. Liquify in a blender and serve over pasta.

makes 8 portions of sauce

tasty liver sticks

This recipe for liver makes good finger food and it's nice and soft for your baby to chew.

⅓ lb calf's liver, trimmed and cut into strips
1 tablespoon flour
Vegetable oil for sautéing
½ onion, peeled and chopped

½ cup button mushrooms, sliced
2 teaspoons tomato purée
¾ cup beef, chicken or vegetable stock (see pages 33–34)

Toss the liver in the flour and brown it in the oil. Don't cook it for long or it will become tough. Remove and set aside. Meanwhile, in the same pan, sauté the onion until soft, then add the mushrooms and cook for 2 minutes. Add the tomato purée, stock and the liver strips and simmer for 10 to 15 minutes. Serve as finger food, chop or purée.

makes 6 portions

my first shepherd's pie

This is one of the best recipes for introducing your baby to red meat. The potato gives it a creamy texture and the vegetables add lots of flavor.

3-4 medium potatoes, peeled and cut into chunks
1-2 tablespoons butter or margarine
3 tablespoons milk
½ onion, peeled and chopped
½ celery stalk, chopped

1 medium carrot, chopped
Oil for sautéing
¼ lb lean ground beef
½ cup canned tomatoes, chopped
½ cup chicken stock

Steam potatoes until tender, then mash them together with the butter and milk. Meanwhile, sauté the onion, celery and carrot in oil for about 10 minutes or until softened. Brown the meat in some more oil and then chop in a food processor to make it softer for your baby to chew. Mix the meat with the tomatoes and sautéed vegetables, add the stock and simmer for about 20 minutes. Combine the meat mixture with the mashed potatoes and chop in a food processor to make it super smooth.

makes 7 portions

my first spaghetti bolognese

A good way to encourage your baby to eat meat is to make a tasty pasta sauce. I cook the pasta until it is nice and soft and I purée the meat sauce to make it very smooth. Scarlett, my one-year-old daughter, loves sucking spaghetti into her mouth and has as much fun playing with it as eating it!

2 oz spaghetti
¼ cup chopped onion
½ red pepper, seeded and chopped
Vegetable oil for sautéing
¼ lb lean ground beef

½ teaspoon tomato purée
2 medium tomatoes, skinned, seeded and chopped
½ cup chicken or vegetable stock (see pages 33–34)

Cook the pasta and cut it up into pieces. Meanwhile, sauté the onion and pepper in the oil until soft. Add the meat and brown it, then add the tomato purée, chopped tomatoes and stock and simmer for about 10 minutes. Chop the meat sauce in a food processor and pour this sauce over the pasta.

makes 3 portions

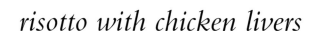

risotto with chicken livers

This is another way of dressing up liver to appeal to children.

⅓ cup brown rice
1 small onion, peeled and chopped
½ small red pepper, seeded and chopped
Vegetable oil for sautéing
2 oz chicken livers, cut into pieces

¼ cup chicken or vegetable stock (see
pages 33–34)
¼ cup apple juice
3 tablespoons frozen peas
1 hard-boiled egg, chopped into pieces

Cook the rice. Meanwhile, sauté the onion and pepper in a little oil until soft, then add the liver and sauté for about 1 minute. Add the stock, apple juice, and the frozen peas and simmer for 4 to 5 minutes. Chop the cooked liver into pieces and add this together with the rest of the peas and pepper mixture to the cooked rice. Finally add the chopped hard-boiled egg.

makes 2 portions

creamy fruit with tofu

Soft tofu has a creamy texture that is appealing to babies; combining dried fruit with tofu lessens the fruit's intense sweetness.

⅓ cup mixed dried fruit
3 oz soft tofu

2 tablespoons yogurt

Cover the fruit with water and simmer for about 10 minutes or until soft. Blend together with the tofu and yogurt.

makes 4 portions

mixed fruit compote

Dried fruits tend to have a laxative effect on babies so I like to mix fresh and dried fruits together. This purée is good mixed with milk and baby rice, crème fraîche, yogurt or sieved cottage cheese.

½ cup mixed dried fruit
1 short cinnamon stick (optional)

2 apples, peeled, cored and cut into pieces
2 pears, peeled, cored and cut into pieces

Put the dried fruit into a saucepan and cover with water (add the cinnamon stick if you like). Simmer the fruit for about 10 minutes, then add the fresh fruit and cook for another 4 minutes. Discard the cinnamon stick and blend the cooked fruit to the desired consistency.

makes 6 portions

creamy apple dessert

This will take only a couple of minutes to prepare. The lemon juice is to keep the apple from turning brown.

1 apple, peeled, cored and grated　　*2 tablespoons yogurt*
Squeeze of lemon juice (optional)　　*1 tablespoon apple juice*
4 chopped raisins

Simply mix all the ingredients together.

makes 2 portions

TODDLERS

MOVING ON

"That's yucky! I'm not eating it" – these words are guaranteed to cut close to any parent's heart; you are a very lucky parent indeed if your toddler enjoys eating and you have never experienced stubbornness, lack of interest or unreasonable fussiness when it comes to mealtimes. So many parents find that at around the age of one their child suddenly changes from being a good eater, enthusiastically anticipating the treats in store as he sits strapped into his high chair, to going on a virtual hunger strike. Life is too exciting to worry about food when you've just learned to walk, and threatening your two-year-old that he won't grow up "big and strong like Daddy" and doing your version of the can-can on the kitchen table will do little to encourage him to eat if he doesn't want to.

After the age of one, a child's weight gain slows down dramatically. Whereas a child might gain 20 lbs in his first year, it is quite normal to gain only 4 or 5 in his second. You'll notice how his chubby baby body slims down as he becomes more active. Health bears little relationship to weight gain; a child's energy level and zest for life are a much better guide. Making a big deal about your child's eating (or not eating) will only steel his resolve.

Most toddlers are just beginning to assert their new-found independence and enjoy engaging their parents in a tough battle of wills. Just when you think you have won and your two-year-old has condescended to pick up a wafer-thin slice of apple that has been sitting on her plate for the last 20 minutes, she suddenly discovers a microscopic blemish on the fruit. In her own inimitable, finicky way, she hurls it on the floor in such a disdainful manner as if to say, "You can't really expect me to eat *that*".

Eventually your child wears you down to such an extent that you can't face cooking for her any more. You no longer care what she eats as long as she eats something. Out come the chips and as you turn your back to open the freezer door and reach for the ice cream, she knows that she has won.

Don't despair; some of the following lines of action will help.

◆ *DON'T GIVE IN!*: You can relax in the knowledge that no child has ever willingly starved himself to death. If your child won't eat his meal, call a halt to the proceedings. Leave some good wholesome food within his reach and when he is hungry, he will eat without any coaxing on your part.

◆ *PEER PRESSURE*: Visit a friend's house where there is a child who likes eating and you may find that your child will eat whatever is offered.

◆ *"HELPING" IN THE KITCHEN*: One of the best ways to encourage children to eat is to involve them in preparing the meal. Children are more likely to taste dishes they've helped to make. Even helping to put away the groceries often arouses curiosity to try new foods.

◆ *VARYING THE VENUE*: You can work wonders by transporting stubborn eaters to the backyard, or simply laying out a picnic on the kitchen floor.

◆ *GIVE AND TAKE*: One of the commonest reasons for fights about food is that children use them to assert their independence. Try negotiating and offer your child a choice – give her three vegetables and let her choose which two she eats.

◆ *LOOKING AND SOUNDING GOOD*: Why not spend a few minutes arranging the food on your child's plate in such a way as to capture his roving eye? (See Fish-shaped salmon cakes or Funny face burgers on pages 87 and 156.) Or make your child a mini portion of his own like a shepherd's pie in a ramekin dish.

Giving dishes names helps too – Goldilocks' Porridge, Mermaid Morsels, Thomas The Tank Engine Minestrone – your four-year-old will be impressed if he thinks he is eating his cartoon character's favorite food.

◆ *EATING WITH YOUR CHILD*: It is a good idea to eat with your child; mealtimes should be enjoyed but there must be a difference between playing and eating. You may be quite happy for a while to play airplanes with fork loads of shepherd's pie and mold mashed potatoes into *Sesame Street* characters, but making a game out of eating may make your child dependent on your personalized service long after your patience has been stretched to its limit. Children are great mimics, so if they see you eating with relish . . .

◆ *COMBINING FOODS*: Try mixing new foods with old favorites. Adding fruit often makes food more appealing (like my recipe for Chicken balls with apples and zucchini on page 119).

◆ *ETHNIC FOODS*: Many ethnic foods are made with healthy ingredients – take a stir-fry, for example, which is full of lovely crisp vegetables. There are some delicious ethnic recipes in this book that are simple to make, like the Indonesian rice dish Nasi goreng (see page 96). To encourage your child to be more adventurous, next time he has his friends over for a meal, lay out a taste table with a selection of unusual foods like chicken yakitori, taramasalata, hummus, satay, and exotic fruits.

◆ *FAST FOOD*: Not all convenience food is bad for children. In the Healthy fast food chapter, I have designed recipes using many of the foods we regularly stock in our kitchen to make delicious simple meals that will appeal to your toddler's fast food inclinations.

EATING OUT

Why is it that when children go to a restaurant they are offered such a limited choice of foods, ones ill-suited to the needs of their growing bodies? Have you ever seen a children's menu that did not offer hot dogs and fries followed by sickly sweet synthetic ice cream? Ask any restaurateur and he'll say it's because that's the food that children like. It's a vicious cycle. Children get used to these over-processed, fatty, artificially flavored and highly colored foods and refuse to eat or even try more natural foods. Parents would be much better off

ordering something simple from the main menu like a pasta dish and letting their child eat some of their food. Mom or Dad's meal is always more enticing anyway and one thing's guaranteed – the more you say, "No, you can't have any of mine," the more they'll want some!

HEALTHY SNACKS

Adults are conditioned into eating three meals a day whether they are hungry or not. Toddlers have more sense and no amount of coaxing will get them to eat when they don't feel like it. I have included plenty of ideas for healthy snacks because many young children get most of their nutrition from the food they eat between meals. Limiting snacks to fruit and raw vegetables and cutting out sweet fruit juices will soon encourage a healthy appetite at mealtimes.

EASY ON THE SALT

When cooking for children, go easy on the salt and never add salt at the table. Whenever possible, use herbs and spices for flavoring instead. Research has shown that a high salt intake can result in high blood pressure and hypertension in adult life.

BRING ON THE BREAKFAST

Breakfast is big business for cereal manufacturers. We are told that children who eat a good breakfast perform better at school and although it can sometimes turn into a battle of wills, we all try to send our children to school with some good nourishing food inside them. However, as far as cereal manufacturers are concerned, there is a conflict between healthy diets and healthy profits. Healthy cereals like Cheerios or corn flakes contain only minimal amounts of sugar, whereas many of the latest "designer" cereals can contain as much as 49 percent sugar. The-once healthy bowl of cereal is looking more and more like a bowl of candy.

These refined cereals are so lacking in nutrients that there need to be long lists of vitamins and minerals added to replace all the goodness lost in the processing. Many mothers reading the long lists of nutritional information on the packets are persuaded that these sugary, vitamin-enriched cereals are good for their children, and children get used to the colorful packaging, novelty gifts and sweet-tasting cereals and come to regard these as real food, refusing anything else.

There are many nutritious grains that can be mixed together to make your own delicious recipes. Wheat germ is particularly good and can be sprinkled onto natural yogurt mixed with some fresh fruit and a little honey. It is easy to make wonderful homemade mueslis combining rolled oats and wheat germ with fresh and dried fruits, coconut and some grated or chopped nuts. This can be mixed with milk, yogurt or fruit juice and sweetened with a little honey if necessary. I've included two of my favorite recipes here but there are endless variations on this theme using whichever fruits happen to be in season. If we can encourage our children to enjoy eating healthy whole-grain cereals from an early age, then hopefully they will reject these sickly, sweet cereals that manufacturers produce especially for children.

Cereals aren't the end of the story either.

With a little imagination your child can enjoy a variety of delicious, healthy breakfasts that will set her up for the day ahead.

HANDY TIPS FOR BETTER BREAKFASTS

◆ Muffins are great for breakfast and you can bake lots of delicious healthy foods inside them. Bake them the day before or you can freeze a batch and take one or two out the night before. (See pages 74, 128, 136 for muffin recipes.)

◆ If your child's a poor eater but tends to be most hungry at breakfast time, give her a cooked breakfast like a vegetable omelette or maybe even offer something from last night's dinner.

◆ Add fresh fruit to packaged breakfast cereals and let your child make his own combinations. Nicholas makes his own "muesli" by mixing corn flakes and other dry cereals, raisins and sliced banana.

◆ Instead of jam, you can make your own fruit spread by mixing dried or fresh fruit purée (see page 30) with crème fraîche, cream or cheese.

◆ If your child doesn't like drinking milk, try hot chocolate or, for lovers of peanut butter, 2 to 3 tablespoons of hot chocolate mix combined with ¾ cup hot milk and blended with a banana and a spoonful of peanut butter. For a treat, use cold milk and add a scoop of chocolate ice cream. Also try delicious milkshakes: 1–2 large pitted dates, 1 banana and ½ cup milk blended together; a small carton of raspberry yogurt, 1 small banana and ½ cup chilled milk; or use raspberries and strawberries, or any favorite canned fruit in natural juice to blend with the milk.

◆ Always try to get your child to eat fresh fruit for breakfast – try different varieties and, if you have time, cut them into interesting shapes and arrange them in a pattern on the plate as this always makes it more enticing.

◆ Buy some miniature, colored paper bags and fill them with a mixture of healthy cereals – you could even put a little surprise gift at the bottom of the bag so that your child has to eat up all her cereal before she can get it!

◆ Make a warming bowl of oatmeal and add chopped fresh fruit to it or even peanut butter and raisins.

◆ Cooked dried fruit mixed with fresh fruit and served with yogurt or crème fraîche can be sprinkled with cereals to make a complete breakfast.

◆ Make scrambled eggs more exciting by mixing in cheese and sautéed tomatoes and green onions.

◆ French toast, sliced bread dipped in a

mixture of beaten egg and milk and sautéed in butter, is delicious for breakfast, particularly if you make it with raisin bread. Because breakfast is often a bit of a rush, you can make several portions in advance, store them in the refrigerator or freezer, and then reheat in a toaster.

rich fruity muesli ❄

This is the type of Swiss-style breakfast to set you up for a day's skiing. It's quite delicious and can be prepared the night before if necessary. You can add lots of different fruits like strawberries or peaches if you wish.

¾ cup rolled oats
1-2 tablespoons toasted wheat germ
1 cup apple juice
2 teaspoons lemon juice
1 large apple, peeled and grated
1 small orange, cut into segments with the pith removed
6 grapes (preferably black), halved and seeded

1 small banana, peeled and sliced
1 heaping tablespoon raisins
2 tablespoons finely chopped hazelnuts (optional)
2 tablespoons vanilla yogurt
2 tablespoons cream (optional)
2 teaspoons honey

Soak the oats and wheat germ in the apple juice for about 30 minutes or overnight. Sprinkle the lemon juice over the grated apple and then simply combine all the ingredients. Decorate with fruit.

makes 3 portions

blissful banana bread

Lovely and moist. Serve plain or buttered – great for breakfast
or lunch boxes.

½ cup butter or margarine
½ cup brown sugar
1 egg
3-4 bananas, mashed
3 tablespoons yogurt
1 teaspoon vanilla extract

2 cups flour
1 tablespoon baking powder
1 teaspoon cinnamon
Pinch of salt
½ cup raisins
¾ cup chopped pecans or walnuts

Preheat the oven to 350°F and grease a 9- x 5-inch loaf pan.
Beat the butter or margarine and sugar together until creamy, then add
the egg and continue to beat until smooth. Add the mashed bananas, yogurt
and vanilla extract. Sift together the flour, baking powder, cinnamon and salt
and beat this gradually into the banana mixture. Finally stir in the raisins and
chopped nuts. Bake for about 1 hour or until a toothpick inserted in the center
comes out clean.

makes 1 loaf

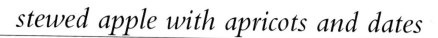

stewed apple with apricots and dates

Adding dried fruit to cooking apples is a way of sweetening them without using sugar. This fruit trio has a wonderful flavor and it is delicious for breakfast as well as after a meal. Serve plain or with crème fraîche, yogurt or custard.

1 large cooking apple
3 large dates
4 dried apricots

6 tablespoons apple juice
4 tablespoons water

Peel, core and chop the apple. Peel off the outer skin of the dates and remove the pits. Chop the dates and apricots. Put the fruit into a saucepan together with the apple juice and water, and simmer for 15 to 20 minutes or until the apples are soft and mushy.

makes 2 portions

VEGETABLE VARIETY

You don't need to be a vegetarian to enjoy vegetable dishes as a main meal. There are lots of delicious recipes to choose from in this section that will encourage your child to like vegetables. You can also adapt some of the recipes in the Baby section – Cinderella's pumpkin (see page 36) and Lettuce, cauliflower and zucchini purée (see page 47) make wonderful soups, and Mock baked beans (see page 49) are a particular favorite with my baby daughter, Scarlett, and my husband, Simon! A selection of raw or steamed vegetables served with a dipping sauce decorated to look like an animal's face is great for birthday parties and can be more intriguing than a plate of chips (see page 129).

Vegetable pasta salads are very popular with children; they love to pick out all the different colored vegetables and pasta shapes, and they are quick to prepare and look very attractive. Stuffed baked potatoes are another favorite – these can be packed with lots of healthy ingredients and are very easy to make. Vegetable quiches can be cut into individual portions and frozen, ready to be used at your convenience. Beans and lentils are inexpensive and you can use them in salads, soups and stews.

The shorter the storage time and the cooler the conditions in which vegetables are kept, the fresher the vegetables and the more nutrients they contain. If possible it is better to shop more often for fresh produce rather than buying in bulk and keeping it lingering in your refrigerator. Interestingly, commercially frozen food is frozen so soon after it is picked that sometimes frozen food can be "fresher" than fresh produce on the shelves. Try to keep all fruit and vegetables loosely wrapped in the refrigerator (although bananas should be stored in a cool pantry) and use as soon as possible.

As the table on the next page shows, frozen vegetables that are not overcooked can be almost as nutritious as fresh vegetables. However, canned peas after cooking have lost most of their vitamin C. The best

	Vitamin C per 100 mg
Fresh **raw** peas	24 mg
Fresh peas **cooked in water**	16 mg
BUT	
Frozen peas **cooked in water**	12 mg
Fresh peas **stored for 4 days** and then cooked	15 mg
AND	
Canned peas after cooking	1 mg

method of cooking to retain as many nutrients as possible is steaming or microwaving. Boiled broccoli retains only 35 percent of its vitamin C as opposed to 72 percent when it is steamed or microwaved. Scrub or wash fruit and vegetables rather than peeling them as most of the vitamins lie just beneath the surface. Also, it is much better to cook vegetables whole whenever possible; they may cook faster if cut into small pieces, but vitamin loss increases.

floating mushroom soup

My daughter Lara loves mushrooms and rice and so I have combined them to make this recipe.

½ lb mushrooms
1 onion, peeled and chopped
2–3 tablespoons butter or margarine
¼ cup flour
6 cups chicken or vegetable stock (see pages 33–34)

1 tablespoon brown rice
1 bay leaf
Salt and freshly ground black pepper
2 tablespoons cream
1 tablespoon chopped fresh chives

Wash the mushrooms, wipe them dry and thinly slice them. Sauté the onion in the butter or margarine until soft, then add the mushrooms. Cover the mushrooms with parchment paper and put a lid over the frying pan. Simmer for about 5 minutes. Stir in the flour and add the stock. Add the rice and bay leaf, bring to a boil and simmer for about 20 minutes. Season with a little salt and pepper and stir in the cream and chives. Remove the bay leaf before serving.

makes 6 portions

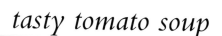

tasty tomato soup

There's something very homey and comforting about a delicious bowl of tomato soup. It's also easy to turn it into a complete meal by adding some cooked rice and diced chicken.

1 medium onion, peeled and sliced
1 medium carrot, washed, scrubbed and sliced
1–2 tablespoons butter
¼ cup flour
2 fresh tomatoes, skinned, seeded and sliced
1 can (14-oz) tomatoes, drained and chopped

2 cups chicken or vegetable stock (see pages 33–34)
1 bay leaf
1 teaspoon sugar
A little salt and freshly ground black pepper
4 tablespoons evaporated milk

Sauté the onion and carrot in butter until soft (about 6 minutes). Stir in the flour, then add the tomatoes, stock, bay leaf, sugar and seasoning. Bring to a boil and simmer for 20 to 30 minutes. Remove the bay leaf and blend the soup until smooth in a food processor. Finally stir in the evaporated milk.

makes 5 portions

onion soup with floating stars

The secret of a good onion soup is long, slow cooking of the onions, which brings out the delicious sweet flavor that children love. The floating stars on top make this soup irresistible! I prefer to use potato rather than flour to thicken the soup.

2–3 onions, peeled and finely sliced
1–2 tablespoons butter or margarine
4 cups chicken or vegetable stock (see pages 33–34)
1 large potato, peeled and cubed

6 slices of bread
Butter or margarine for spreading
6 slices of Swiss or Gruyère cheese
A little freshly ground black pepper

Toss the onions in the butter or margarine melted in a large casserole. Cover and cook gently for 30 to 40 minutes, letting the onions stew in their own juices until soft. Remove the lid, turn up the heat, and cook the onions, stirring occasionally, until lightly browned. Meanwhile put the stock into a saucepan with the potato and simmer for about 10 minutes or until the potato is soft. Blend the potato and chicken stock in a blender.

Pour the thickened chicken stock over the onions and simmer gently, uncovered, for 20 to 30 minutes. Spread some bread with butter or margarine and put a slice of the cheese on top. Cut out shapes with a star-shaped cookie cutter and put these under the broiler until the cheese has melted. Season and place a star on the top of each bowl of soup. (You can also add a teaspoon of grated cheese to each bowl of soup.)

makes 6 portions

chopped cobb salad ❄

We spent a magical Christmas holiday in Disneyworld, Florida. This salad recipe is the speciality at The Brown Derby Restaurant in the MGM studio complex, where we ate on several occasions. Traditionally, the salad is made with blue cheese and bacon. I have removed the bacon from my recipe because it's high in fat, and you could substitute a different cheese, for example, Swiss, in place of the blue cheese if your child prefers it. The meat is also optional. The chopped avocado should not be added to the salad until just before it is served or it will turn brown.

1 hard-boiled egg
2 tablespoons Roquefort cheese
1 small head iceberg lettuce
⅓ cup cooked turkey or chicken breast (optional)
1 tablespoon balsamic or red wine vinegar

2 tablespoons olive oil
Pinch of sugar
1 tablespoon chopped chives or green onion
Salt and freshly ground black pepper
½ avocado, chopped

Finely chop the egg, Roquefort, lettuce and turkey or chicken (if using) and put into a bowl. Prepare the dressing by whisking the vinegar into the oil, followed by the sugar and chives or green onion. Season lightly. Just before eating chop the avocado flesh and add to the ingredients in the bowl before adding the dressing.

makes 3 portions

twice-baked potatoes

Stuffed twice-baked potatoes make a delicious meal served with a salad or perhaps raw vegetables and a dip (see pages 129–131).

2 large potatoes
Oil for brushing
Salt
2 tablespoons soft cream cheese
½ cup grated Mozzarella cheese
3 tablespoons grated Parmesan cheese

¼ cup grated Cheddar cheese
1 tomato, skinned, seeded and chopped
2 green onions, finely chopped
Salt and freshly ground black pepper
A little extra grated Cheddar cheese for sprinkling

Preheat the oven to 400°F. Prick the skin of the potatoes and brush them with oil and sprinkle with a little salt. Bake for 1¼ hours or until soft. Halve the potatoes lengthwise, scoop out the flesh into a bowl and mash together with the cheeses, tomato, green onions and seasoning.

Spoon the mixture back into the potato shells and sprinkle with the extra grated Cheddar cheese. Bake for another 10 to 15 minutes or until golden.

makes 4 portions

zucchini and potato muffins

The shape and size of a muffin is very appealing to children; these savory muffins are crispy on the outside and lovely and moist when you bite into them. They are a great favorite in Nicholas's lunch box. As a variation, you could add grated Cheddar or Gruyère cheese.

3 medium potatoes, peeled and grated
1 large or 2 medium zucchini, washed and grated
1 medium onion, peeled and grated

1 egg, lightly beaten
2 tablespoons flour
¼ cup melted butter or margarine
Salt and freshly ground black pepper

Preheat the oven to 350°F.
Squeeze out any excess liquid from the grated vegetables and mix together with the egg, flour, butter or margarine and a little seasoning. Spoon the mixture into a muffin pan lined with paper liners (the mixture will stick badly without the liners). Bake for about 35 minutes until crispy and golden.

makes 10 muffins

rice is nice

⅓ cup brown rice
2 eggs, separated
1–2 tablespoons melted butter or margarine
¾ cup milk

1 cup grated Swiss cheese
Salt and freshly ground black pepper
2 medium tomatoes, sliced
1 tablespoon grated Parmesan

Preheat the oven to 350°F.
Cook the rice according to the instructions on the package. Beat the egg yolks and mix with the butter or margarine, milk and cheese. Season and stir into the cooked rice. Beat the egg whites until stiff and fold them into the egg and rice mixture. Pour into a greased glass ovenproof dish and top with the sliced tomatoes. Sprinkle with the Parmesan and bake for about 30 minutes.

makes 3 portions

sesame tofu sticks ❄

Tofu can taste very bland but left to soak in this marinade it takes on a delicious flavor. A crisp sesame seed coating on the outside combines well with the soft tofu. Don't be alarmed at the use of the sake and honey – most of the marinade won't actually be eaten and, anyway, the alcohol is evaporated during cooking! These make a delicious meal served with noodles and stir-fried vegetables.

10½ oz firm tofu
2 tablespoons soy sauce
2 tablespoons sake or dry sherry
(optional)
1 tablespoon honey

¼ small onion, peeled and chopped
Whole-wheat flour for coating
Sesame seeds for coating
Vegetable oil for sautéing

Carefully drain the liquid from the tofu and cut into domino-shaped pieces. Combine the soy sauce, sake or sherry (if using), honey and onion and marinate the tofu in the mixture overnight or for at least 2 hours. When you are ready to eat, coat the tofu in a mixture of flour and sesame seeds and sauté in hot oil until browned (about 4 minutes). Serve hot or cold.

makes 3 portions

cheese, onion and tomato tart

This is a delicious tart and can be served hot or cold. It can be frozen in individual portions for your child and reheated in the oven. It's a good addition to your child's lunch box. If you prefer, use frozen whole-wheat pastry instead of making your own.

1 cup whole-wheat flour
1 teaspoon baking powder
½ cup butter or margarine
3 tablespoons finely grated Parmesan
cheese
A pinch of dry mustard
A pinch of salt
½ beaten egg
2 tablespoons cold water

3 onions, peeled and sliced
3 eggs
3 tablespoons milk or cream
A little freshly grated nutmeg
Salt and freshly ground black pepper
1½ cups grated Cheddar cheese
4 medium tomatoes, washed and thinly
sliced

To make the pastry, put the flour and baking powder in a bowl and rub in half of the butter or margarine until the mixture resembles crumbs. Add the Parmesan, mustard and salt. Make a well in the center, add the beaten egg and water, and knead to make a firm dough. Wrap in plastic film and refrigerate for at least 30 minutes.

Preheat the oven to 400°F. Roll out the pastry on a lightly floured board and line a greased 8-inch tart pan. Prick the base all over with a fork, line with parchment paper, fill with dried beans and bake blind (i.e., without the filling) for about 10 minutes.

Meanwhile to prepare the filling, sauté the onions in the remaining butter or margarine over low heat until soft but not browned. Beat the eggs together with the milk or cream, add a little nutmeg and season lightly with salt and pepper. Stir in the Cheddar cheese.

Lay the onions over the base of the tart, pour in the cheese mixture and arrange the sliced tomatoes on top. Bake for 30 minutes at 400°F or until the filling has set.

makes 6 portions

tasty tofu and peanut butter stir-fry ❊

Tofu is high in protein and low in fat. It is very versatile
and soft to chew. There are two types of tofu; one is very soft (called
"silken") and the other more solid ("firm"). This tasty recipe goes down
very well with my kids, and adults love it too!

2 tablespoons dark soy sauce
2 tablespoons smooth peanut butter
1 teaspoon brown sugar
2 oz thin egg noodles
4 tablespoons sesame oil
1 lb firm tofu, cut into ½-inch cubes
and rolled in flour
2 green onions, finely sliced
1 small head Chinese cabbage, washed
and shredded
1 cup bean sprouts

Mix together the soy sauce, peanut butter and sugar. Cook the noodles according to the directions on the package and set aside. In a wok or frying pan heat 3 tablespoons of the oil, and sauté the tofu until golden brown on all sides (about 5 minutes). Heat the remaining oil in another frying pan and sauté the green onions for 1 minute; add the cabbage and bean sprouts and continue to cook for 2 to 3 minutes.

Add the tofu, noodles and peanut sauce. Mix thoroughly and cook over low heat for a couple of minutes.

makes 4 portions

ravishing risotto

To make a traditional risotto is very time-consuming; liquid is added to the rice about four times during the cooking period. Anyone with children to look after will know that cooking something that involves a lot of attention and precise timing can quickly result in a very burnt saucepan. With this recipe the liquid is added all at once and the rice can be left to simmer in a covered saucepan for 40 minutes quite happily. You can add all kinds of vegetables to this basic risotto – just lightly sauté leeks, mushrooms, red peppers, zucchini or your child's favorite vegetable, and add with the Parmesan.

1 large onion, peeled and finely chopped
2–3 tablespoons butter or margarine
1 ¼ cups brown rice
4 cups chicken or vegetable stock (see pages 33–34)

⅔ cup frozen peas
¾ cup freshly grated Parmesan cheese
¼ teaspoon freshly grated nutmeg
Freshly ground black pepper

Sauté the onion in the butter or magarine over medium heat in a heavy casserole until soft (about 5 minutes). Rinse the rice thoroughly under cold running water, add to the onion and stir with a wooden spoon until well coated with butter. Add the chicken or vegetable stock, bring to a boil, then cover and leave to simmer over low heat for about 45 minutes (check from time to time and add extra stock if necessary). Add the frozen peas 5 minutes before the end. At the end of the cooking time there will still be some liquid left in the rice. Add the Parmesan, nutmeg and a little pepper and stir very well for a couple of minutes. If left to stand, the excess liquid will soon be absorbed by the warm rice. Sprinkle with extra Parmesan if desired.

makes 5 portions

PERFECT PASTA

Most children adore pasta. It's fun to eat and easy to chew. Fresh-cooked pasta in a myriad of different shapes, colors and sizes, served with a delicious homemade sauce made from fresh natural ingredients makes a quick, easy and inexpensive meal for the whole family. Pasta combines well with almost any food. Children can be enticed to eat lots of different nutritious foods they might never touch were they not served with pasta.

There is a wonderful variety of pasta to choose from. You can buy fresh ravioli stuffed with ricotta and spinach and serve it with a homemade tomato sauce. You can stuff cannelloni with chicken, vegetables or meat. In my local supermarket I can buy pasta in the shape of space ships, animals or cars, and you can even teach your child to read by serving alphabet pasta.

Individual pieces of pasta like fusilli (spirals) or penne (tubes) are easier for young children to eat than long strands of spaghetti. However, my three-year-old daughter has invented her own method of coping with spaghetti – she holds it out in front of her by the two ends, bites in the middle and sucks both ends into her mouth. Not the height of good manners perhaps, but certainly very effective!

pasta with chicken and peppers au gratin

Chicken with pasta is quite unusual, but this creamy pasta with a golden, bubbly topping makes a great combination.

1 chicken breast, cut into small strips
Salt and freshly ground black pepper
Vegetable oil or margarine for sautéing
½ small red pepper, seeded and cut into strips
½ small yellow pepper, seeded and cut into strips

1–2 tablespoons butter or margarine
¼ cup flour
1 cup milk
⅓ cup grated Parmesan cheese
2 oz thin dried spaghetti or fresh pasta

Season the chicken with a little salt and pepper and sauté for about 2 minutes in the oil or margarine. Add the peppers and sauté together with the chicken for 3 to 4 minutes until the chicken is cooked through.

To prepare the sauce, melt the butter or margarine and stir in the flour over low heat, stirring constantly for 2 to 3 minutes. Take the pan off the heat and vigorously stir in the milk. When the sauce is well blended, stir over medium heat until it is thick and smooth. Remove from heat; stir in half of the Parmesan cheese and season lightly with salt and pepper (remember the cheese will already make the sauce quite salty).

Cook the pasta in a large pan of boiling water but leave it a little undercooked as it will be cooked again when it is placed under the broiler. Drain well and mix with the chicken, peppers and cheese sauce; put mixture into an ovenproof dish. Sprinkle the remaining cheese over the top of the pasta and place under a hot broiler for a few minutes until the topping is brown and bubbly.

makes 2 portions

tasty tomato sauce for pasta

Pasta with tomato sauce is always popular with children, and this recipe for
tomato sauce can be used as the basis for many different pasta dishes. It's
worth making this sauce in a large quantity and then freezing it in small
portions. For a tasty variation, sauté a chopped pepper with the onion and
add a small eggplant (sliced into rounds) and lightly sautéed. Then purée
the sauce for a few seconds in a food processor. Combined with a basic
white sauce and some Parmesan cheese it also makes a lovely cream sauce.

1 small onion, peeled and finely
chopped
1 clove garlic, finely chopped (optional)
1 tablespoon finely chopped fresh
parsley
1 tablespoon olive oil
3 tomatoes, skinned, seeded and
chopped (optional)

1 can (28 oz) tomatoes, drained and
chopped
2 tablespoons tomato purée
1 tablespoon fresh basil leaves
¼ teaspoon dried oregano
Salt and freshly ground black pepper

Sauté the onion, garlic (if using) and parsley in the olive oil until soft but not
browned (about 5 minutes). Add the rest of the ingredients and cook over
low heat for about 15 minutes.

makes about 1½ cups sauce

fettuccine with haddock, cheese and tomato

This is a great recipe for encouraging your child to eat more fish. You
could use other white fish like hake or cod instead of haddock.

½–¾ lb haddock
Salt and freshly ground black pepper
Knob of butter or margarine
1 tablespoon lemon juice
1 small onion, peeled and finely sliced
1 tablespoon chopped fresh parsley
⅓ cup cooked frozen or fresh peas
(optional)
3 medium tomatoes, peeled and sliced

2 tablespoons tomato purée
1½ tablespoons butter or margarine
1½ tablespoons flour
1 cup milk
¼ teaspoon freshly grated nutmeg
½ cup grated Cheddar cheese
4 oz spinach fettuccine
1½ tablespoons grated Parmesan cheese

To cook the fish, place it in a microwave dish, season lightly, dot with butter or margarine and sprinkle with lemon juice. Lay the onion slices on top and sprinkle with parsley. Microwave on full power for 5 minutes, turning the fish halfway through. Alternatively, bake the fish and onion in an ovenproof dish at 350°F for 10–15 minutes. Check to make sure the fish is cooked through, then flake with a fork, removing any bones. Mix the flaked fish, onions, parsley, peas (if using) and cooking liquid with the sliced tomatoes and tomato purée.

While the fish is cooking prepare the cheese sauce. Melt the butter or margarine in a saucepan and stir in the flour to make a roux. Let it cook for 1 minute. Gradually stir in the milk to make a thick white sauce and season with nutmeg. Remove from heat; stir in the cheese.

Preheat the oven to 350°F. Cook the pasta in a large pan of boiling water (but leave it a little under done as it will be cooked again in the oven). Drain well and mix with the cheese sauce. In a greased ovenproof dish, put a layer of pasta followed by a layer of fish in tomato sauce. Repeat until all the ingredients have been used. Sprinkle the top with Parmesan. Cook for 10 minutes and then brown under a hot broiler for a couple of minutes.

makes 4 portions

FABULOUS FISH

Fish is a wonderful food for children; it's high in protein, low in fat, has a nice soft texture for lazy chewers and it's quick to cook. It's a shame that many children are confirmed fish-haters. My theory is that often children aren't given the chance to develop a liking for fish and have maybe been put off by being given bland or overcooked fish. Once a child decides he doesn't like a particular food, it's hard to persuade him otherwise.

I have tried to put together a collection of tasty fish recipes to encourage children to be excited at the prospect of fish for dinner. Many of the recipes combine fish with favorite foods like Fish-shaped salmon cakes with tasty tomato sauce (see page 87), fruity fish (see page 86) combining fish fillets with bananas and grapes, and many more. There are several fish recipes in other sections of this book, including ideas for combining pasta with fish and even a recipe for fish stick pie!

Don't forget to flake fish carefully before giving it to your child to make sure there are no bones.

mermaid morsels

I tell my children that these miniature fish balls are Ariel's favorite food –
Ariel being the mermaid in the Disney film *Little Mermaid*. I think this
recipe is one of the tastiest ways of giving your child fish. If you freeze
these once they are cooked, you can simply remove as many as you need
and let them defrost for a delicious meal. Best served cold. You can use
any combination of whatever white fish is available – cod, haddock, whiting,
hake or halibut. A fishmonger should be able to prepare it for you. A
variation to try: Leave out the coating of flour and simmer the balls in the
Tasty tomato sauce for pasta on page 82 for a really scrumptious meal.

2 onions, peeled and finely chopped
Vegetable oil and butter or margarine for
sautéing
2 lb ground or finely chopped white fish
1 large carrot, scrubbed and finely
chopped
1 Granny Smith apple, peeled and
grated

1 tablespoon finely chopped fresh
parsley (optional)
2 eggs
2 tablespoons sugar
2 teaspoons salt
¼ teaspoon freshly ground black pepper
⅓ cup cold water
2 tablespoons flour plus extra for rolling

Sauté the onions in a mixture of oil and butter or margarine until soft and
golden (about 6–7 minutes). Combine ground fish, onions, carrot,
grated apple and parsley (if using). Beat the eggs with the sugar, salt and pepper,
using an electric mixer, until frothy and add the egg mixture to the ground fish.
Finally, mix in the cold water and flour.

Form into small balls, roll in flour and sauté in a mixture of vegetable oil and
butter or margarine until golden.

makes about 40 balls

flaked fish with bananas and grapes

Blending fruit with fish gives it a taste children love. This is quick and easy to make and lovely served over a bed of rice.

½ lb haddock, hake or cod, cut into chunks
Salt and freshly ground black pepper
Butter or margarine for sautéing
2 bananas

10 seedless grapes, peeled
1 tablespoon butter or margarine
1 tablespoon flour
⅔ cup milk

S eason the fish with a little salt and pepper. Sauté the fish in butter or margarine until it flakes easily with a fork. Meanwhile, peel the bananas and cut them in half lengthwise and in half again. Sauté them in butter until soft and golden. Combine the fish, bananas and grapes. Make a white sauce in the usual way (see page 47), season with a little salt and pepper and pour sauce over the fish. Simmer for 4 to 5 minutes. Serve over a bed of rice.

makes 3 portions

fish-shaped salmon cakes

This is a simple way to turn fish cakes into a special treat. They are good surrounded by a red sea of Tasty tomato sauce for pasta (see page 82).

2 medium potatoes
½ lb salmon fillets or
1 can (7 oz) salmon or tuna
Salt and freshly ground black pepper
Squeeze of lemon juice
A few sprigs of parsley
A knob of butter
2 tablespoons ketchup

A few drops of Worcestershire sauce (optional)
1 heaping teaspoon finely chopped fresh chives or green onion
1 egg, beaten
Crushed corn flakes for coating the fish
Vegetable oil

Peel the potatoes, cut into pieces and steam until soft. Set aside until cool. To cook the salmon, preheat the oven to 350°F, place the fillets in foil, season lightly with salt and pepper, add lemon juice and parsley and dot with the butter. Wrap loosely and bake for 15 to 20 minutes. Alternatively, cook the salmon in a microwave in a dish covered with plastic film. (Cook on full power for 3½ to 4½ minutes, turning halfway through.)

Remove the skin from the salmon, drain away any juices and mash with a fork, taking care to remove any bones. Alternatively, flake the canned fish. Add the potato and mash this together with the fish, ketchup, Worcestershire sauce (if using), chives or green onion.

With floured hands, form the mixture into 6 oval fish cakes, then pinch in one end to form the tail of a fish. Brush with beaten egg and roll in the crushed corn flakes. Lightly fry or place on a greased baking sheet, brush with oil and bake for 20–25 minutes, turning after about 10 minutes.

makes 6 fish cakes

salmon kedgeree

I use fresh salmon for this recipe but you could substitute canned salmon or smoked haddock. I use an ice cream scoop to make "castles" of kedgeree for my children and they love it.

¾ cup rice
⅓ lb fresh salmon
1–2 tablespoons butter or margarine
Squeeze of lemon juice
½ small onion, peeled and chopped
1 tablespoon flour
1 cup milk

½ bay leaf
¼ teaspoon grated nutmeg
1 teaspoon mild curry powder
Salt and freshly ground black pepper
1 or 2 hard-boiled eggs, chopped
2 tomatoes, skinned, seeded and chopped

Cook the rice in boiling, lightly salted water until tender. Drain and set aside. Meanwhile, put the fish in a dish, dot with half of the butter or margarine and sprinkle with lemon juice. Cover with plastic film and microwave on full power for 4 to 5 minutes, turning halfway through. Alternatively wrap the fish loosely in foil and bake for about 15 minutes at 350°F.

To prepare the sauce, melt the remaining butter or margarine and sauté the onion until soft. Stir in the flour to make a roux and cook for 1 minute. Gradually add the milk, stirring until the sauce thickens. Add the bay leaf, nutmeg, curry powder and salt and pepper, and simmer for a couple of minutes. Flake the salmon, taking care to remove any bones, and add the fish to the sauce, having first removed the bay leaf. Stir in the chopped hard-boiled egg(s), chopped tomato and cooked rice.

makes 5 portions

fish with tomatoes and cheese

Bringing these packets of scrumptious fish to the table will certainly arouse your child's curiosity. Serve with mashed potatoes or rice. You can use haddock, cod, hake or sole. For a simple but very delicious variation, take a fillet of fish, sprinkle with 1 tablespoon of chopped green onion, 1 tablespoon of soy sauce and dot with butter or margarine. Wrap in foil and cook as below.

½ lb fillets of fish
Salt and freshly ground black pepper
4 medium tomatoes, skinned, seeded
and chopped or 1 can (14 oz) tomatoes,
drained

½ cup grated Cheddar cheese
½ cup corn flakes, crushed
2 tablespoons milk
A knob of butter or margarine

Preheat the oven to 350°F.
  Place the fillets on foil and lightly season. Mix together the tomatoes, cheese, corn flakes and milk and cover each of the fillets with some of the sauce. Dot with margarine and wrap up into separate packets (use parchment paper instead if cooking in the microwave) and cook in the oven for about 15 minutes or for about 4 minutes on full power in a microwave. The fish will flake easily with a fork when cooked. Make sure there are no stray bones, mash the fish together with the sauce and serve.

makes 4 portions

tuna with seashells

Tuna is inexpensive and nutritious — it's worth keeping a can on hand for emergencies. This tasty recipe is popular and quick to make. Finish off with cheese on top or leave plain. If your child is not too keen on tuna, then resort to disguise and purée the sauce in a food processor.

1 cup multicolored pasta shells
1 onion, peeled and finely chopped
1 clove garlic, peeled and crushed
Olive oil for sautéing
½ red and ½ green pepper, seeded and chopped

1 can (14 oz) tomatoes, drained and chopped
2 tablespoons tomato purée
½ teaspoon dried oregano
1 can (7 oz) tuna, drained and flaked
2 tablespoons cream or milk
⅓ cup grated Cheddar cheese

Cook the pasta in boiling water until cooked but firm. Sauté the onion and garlic in the olive oil until soft, then add the peppers and sauté for 2–3 minutes. Add the chopped tomatoes, tomato purée and oregano; bring to a boil and simmer for about 4 minutes. Add the tuna, heat through and then mix in the cream. Place the pasta in an ovenproof dish, add the sauce and sprinkle the Cheddar cheese on top. Brown under a preheated broiler, taking care not to burn the top.

makes 3–4 portions

CHOMPING CHICKEN

Chicken is the staple diet of my family. It is inexpensive, low in fat and so versatile that you could eat chicken almost every day of the week and still not be bored with it. Chicken or turkey offers the same high-quality protein as meat. It is also a good source of vitamin B, which promotes growth, energy, healthy skin and keeps the nervous system in balance. The dark meat of chicken supplies the most iron. The subtle flavor of moist tender chicken can be combined with other foods to appeal to almost every taste.

Diced chicken can be stir-fried in 5 minutes and a boneless breast of chicken takes no more than about 8 minutes to cook. However, chicken should never be served undercooked; make sure that the meat is opaque and white. If the chicken is properly cooked, then it should be tender and bursting with juices.

Plain roast chicken served with a good sauce and roast potatoes is always a family favorite in my house, and I've given a few recipes for using up leftover cold chicken. Children love to chew on chicken drumsticks, but watch young children to make sure that they do not choke on small pieces of bone. You can combine chicken with fruit, rice, vegetables or pasta. Why not tempt your child with one of the more unusual recipes like Nasi goreng (on page 96), an Indonesian recipe combining chicken with rice and peanuts?

tasty chicken stir-fry

Both my older children love stir-fried chicken. Everything is cut into small bite-sized pieces and they like picking out the tender chunks of chicken and the brightly colored vegetables. There are many different vegetable combinations that you can use, and this recipe will provide the basis of many different dishes. As a shortcut you can buy a package of precut stir-fry vegetables in most supermarkets and add a few of your child's favorite vegetables.

2 boneless chicken breasts
2 tablespoons soy sauce
1 teaspoon sugar
1 tablespoon sesame or vegetable oil
2 tablespoons sake or dry sherry (optional)
2 green onions, finely sliced
Freshly ground black pepper
1 cup chicken or vegetable stock (see pages 33–34)
2 tablespoons apple juice
1 tablespoon cornstarch
4 tablespoons vegetable oil

1 onion, peeled and cut into thin slices
1 small green pepper and 1 small red pepper, seeded and cut into strips
1 cup cauliflower florets
1 cup sliced green beans
¾ cup shredded cabbage
8 ears of baby sweet corn, cut in half
1 cup chicken or vegetable stock (see pages 33–34) (optional)
4 oz thin Chinese noodles (optional)
2 tablespoons sesame seeds, toasted in an ungreased frying pan.

Cut the chicken breasts into bite-sized pieces. Combine the soy sauce, sugar, oil, sake or sherry (if using), green onions and a little pepper and marinate the chicken in this mixture for at least 1 hour. To make a sauce, heat the stock in a saucepan. Mix the apple juice with the cornstarch until it has completely dissolved. Add this to the stock and simmer until thickened.

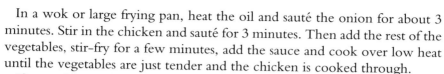

In a wok or large frying pan, heat the oil and sauté the onion for about 3 minutes. Stir in the chicken and sauté for 3 minutes. Then add the rest of the vegetables, stir-fry for a few minutes, add the sauce and cook over low heat until the vegetables are just tender and the chicken is cooked through.

If you wish to add noodles, bring 1 cup stock (or just use water) to a boil, stir in the noodles, cover the pan and allow to simmer for 3 minutes, gently stirring with a fork from time to time. Drain and mix the noodles with the chicken and vegetables and sprinkle with the sesame seeds.

makes 4 portions

chicken drumsticks with barbecue sauce

Chicken drumsticks are fun for your child to hold and eat. Simply wrap the ends in foil and they can be eaten either hot or cold.

½ small onion, finely chopped
Margarine or oil for sautéing
1 teaspoon lemon juice
2 teaspoons malt or rice vinegar
1 teaspoon brown sugar

2 tablespoons tomato purée
A few drops of Worcestershire sauce
Salt and freshly ground black pepper
2 chicken drumsticks

Sauté the onion in the margarine or oil until soft, then stir in the lemon juice, vinegar, sugar, tomato purée and Worcestershire sauce. Simmer gently for 3 to 4 minutes and season lightly. Remove the skin from the drumsticks, make 2 deep cuts in each and brush all over with the sauce. Place on a piece of foil and cook under a preheated broiler for about 20 minutes, turning frequently and basting with the sauce.

makes 2 portions

chicken and potato pancake

A delicious thick golden crispy pancake with a soft succulent center. This recipe can be varied by adding other vegetables like grated zucchini or chopped sweet peppers. I make it in a 6-inch frying pan and my children enjoy cutting their own wedges – it can be eaten either hot or cold.

*1 chicken breast, cut into pieces or some
leftover cooked chicken
1¼ cups chicken or vegetable stock (see
pages 33–34)
1 baking potato, peeled and grated
1 onion, peeled and grated*

*¼ cup frozen peas
1 small egg, beaten
1 tablespoon flour
Salt and freshly ground black pepper
2 tablespoons vegetable oil*

Poach the chicken breast in the stock until cooked through (15–20 minutes). Press out the liquid from the grated potato and combine the potato with the onion, frozen peas, egg and flour; season lightly with salt and pepper. Dice the chicken and add it to the vegetable mixture.

Heat 1 tablespoon of oil in the frying pan, tilt the pan so that the oil coats the sides, and press the mixture into the pan. Sauté for about 5 minutes or until browned. Turn the pancake onto a plate. Heat the rest of the oil in the pan and brown the pancake on the other side. Cut into wedges.

makes 4 portions

sweet and sour chicken

Sweet and sour chicken is a great favorite with young children; this sauce is also very good with fish. Serve on a bed of rice.

Salt and freshly ground black pepper
3 chicken breasts, cut in half
Vegetable oil for sautéing
1 large onion, peeled and finely chopped
1 green pepper, seeded and cut into fine strips
1 red pepper, seeded and cut into fine strips

1½ tablespoons cider vinegar or red wine vinegar
2 tablespoons tomato purée
1 can (5 oz) pineapple chunks in syrup
1¼ cups water
2 tablespoons soy sauce
½ teaspoon ground ginger (optional)
1 tablespoon cornstarch

Preheat the oven to 350°F.

Season the chicken breasts lightly and sauté in the oil until lightly browned. Drain on paper towels.

Sauté the onion in a little oil for 3 to 4 minutes, then add the peppers and continue to cook for another 2 minutes; set aside.

Combine the vinegar, tomato purée, ¼ cup pineapple syrup from the can of pineapple, water, soy sauce and ginger (if using) and stir until well mixed. Put the chicken breasts into a casserole dish, cover with this mixture, and stir in the onion and peppers. Bake the chicken for 20 minutes. Add the pineapple chunks and bake for another 10 minutes. Remove the chicken and pour the sauce into a saucepan. Mix the cornstarch with a little cold water and stir this into the sauce; bring to a boil and simmer until the sauce is thickened.

Remove the chicken from the bone, cut it into small pieces and cover with the sauce.

makes 6 portions

nasi goreng

This is a delicious Indonesian rice recipe flavored with peanuts and a mild curry sauce. It is a great favorite with the whole family.

2 chicken breasts, skinned and boned,
cut into chunks
3 tablespoons soy sauce
¼ cup sesame or vegetable oil
1 large onion, peeled and finely chopped
2 teaspoons curry powder
½ teaspoon turmeric
1½ cups basmati rice
3 cups chicken or vegetable stock (see
pages 33–34)

Vegetable oil for frying
3 green onions, finely chopped
1 red pepper, seeded and finely chopped
¾ cup baby sweet corn, cut in half
lengthwise
½ cup frozen peas
1 tablespoon molasses
½ cup roasted peanuts, finely chopped

Marinate the chicken in the soy sauce for at least 1 hour. In a large saucepan heat the oil, add the onion, curry powder and turmeric and sauté for 5 minutes. Add the rice and continue to stir and cook for another 5 minutes until it has turned golden. Add the stock and simmer, covered, for 20 to 25 minutes or until the rice is tender.

Meanwhile in a wok or saucepan, fry the chicken in the vegetable oil for about 3 minutes. Add the green onions, red pepper, baby sweet corn and the soy sauce from the chicken marinade. Cook the vegetables for about 2 minutes, then add the frozen peas. Continue cooking for another 3 to 4 minutes. Combine the chicken and vegetables with the rice and stir in the molasses and chopped peanuts. Simmer for about 5 minutes.

makes 8 portions

Florentine chicken strips

This dish freezes well, so I usually make 3 or 4 individual portions from this recipe. As a variation you could add sliced button mushrooms sautéed in a little butter to the sauce.

3 chicken breasts, cut into strips
Salt and freshly ground black pepper
3–4 tablespoons butter or margarine
1 lb fresh spinach
1½ tablespoons flour

1¼ cups chicken or vegetable stock (see
pages 33–34)
½ cup cream or milk
½ cup grated Cheddar cheese
¼ teaspoon grated nutmeg
3 tablespoons grated Parmesan cheese

Preheat the oven to 350°F.
Season the chicken with a little salt and pepper and sauté in half of the butter or margarine for 3 to 4 minutes. Meanwhile cook the spinach and squeeze out the excess water. Put the spinach into a greased ovenproof dish and place the strips of chicken on top.

To make the sauce, melt the remaining butter or margarine, add the flour and cook for 1 minute. Gradually add the chicken or vegetable stock, stirring constantly to make a thick sauce. Bring to a boil, then remove from the heat. Stir in the cream or milk, Cheddar cheese and grated nutmeg; season with a little salt and pepper. Pour this sauce over the chicken and sprinkle with Parmesan. Cook in the oven for 10 minutes.

makes 3–4 portions

cold chicken with sweet curry sauce ❄

This is my favorite recipe for using up leftover chicken. It's great served with rice, and my children like it when I cut the chicken into cubes and thread the pieces onto skewers.

½ onion, peeled and chopped
1 tablespoon corn oil
2 teaspoons curry powder
1½ tablespoons apricot jam
1 teaspoon lemon juice
¼ cup chicken or vegetable stock (see pages 33–34)

½ teaspoon tomato purée
1 bay leaf
½ cup mayonnaise
1 tablespoon raisins
1½ cups cooked chicken pieces, cut into chunks

Sauté the onion in the oil until soft and add the curry powder. Simmer for 1 minute, then stir in the apricot jam and lemon juice and cook gently for 1 minute more. Pour in the stock, add the tomato purée and the bay leaf and simmer for about 4 minutes. Remove from heat, take out the bay leaf and beat in the mayonnaise. Stir in the raisins and pour the sauce over the chicken.

makes 4 portions

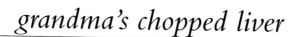

grandma's chopped liver

There is a tendency for parents who dislike liver not to make it for their children, but you should not show your dislike of certain foods because your child will be inclined to mimic you. It is better for your child to experiment for himself and make his own choices.

This is a tasty way of making liver for your child; spread it onto fingers or mini-triangles of toast and sprinkle with the chopped egg. It can also be used for sandwich fillings. I make it in bulk and then freeze it in small portions; it comes in handy as a nutritious meal or snack.

1 medium onion, peeled and finely chopped
2 tablespoons vegetable oil

½ lb chicken livers
2 hard-boiled eggs, chopped
Salt and freshly ground black pepper

Sauté the onion in the oil until golden. Meanwhile broil the chicken livers until cooked through (about 5 minutes). Mix with 1½ of the chopped eggs, keeping the remainder for garnish, and season to taste with a little salt and pepper.

makes 8 portions

super chicken satay

Satay is a natural for peanut-butter lovers and it's a great sauce for beef, prawns or chicken. Of course, eating food off a stick is always very appealing to children, so this recipe is a real winner.

2 large chicken breasts
½ cup chicken stock
⅓ cup crunchy peanut butter
1 teaspoon soy sauce
1 tablespoon sake or sherry

1 tablespoon honey
1 teaspoon curry powder
½ teaspoon turmeric
2 tablespoons onion, finely chopped
1 small clove garlic, crushed

Cut the chicken breasts into chunks. Mix all the rest of the ingredients together to make the sauce; bring it to a boil and simmer for 5 minutes. Marinate the chicken in the sauce for several hours or refrigerate and leave overnight. Thread three or four pieces of chicken onto each skewer and broil or barbecue them for 20 minutes or until cooked, turning frequently and basting occasionally with the sauce.

makes 6 skewers

Nicholas's chicken on a stick ✳

My son Nicholas loves this recipe. The chicken pieces are deliciously
moist and very appealing if you thread them onto bamboo skewers with chunks
of steamed baby corn and red pepper in between.

For the mild curry dip
½ small onion, peeled and chopped
vegetable oil
½ tablespoon mild curry powder
1 teaspoon brown sugar
1 tablespoon flour
½ cup chicken stock (see page 33)

2 chicken breasts
1 egg white
1 tablespoon light soy sauce
1 tablespoon sake or sherry
1 tablespoon cornstarch
sesame or vegetable oil

To make the dip, sauté the onion until soft. Stir in the curry powder and
sugar. Add the flour and continue stirring, gradually adding the chicken
stock until thickened.

Cut the chicken diagonally into strips, or into chunks if you are going to
thread it onto a skewer. Whisk together the egg white, soy sauce, sake and
cornstarch; add the chicken and mix well. Heat the oil in a wok or frying pan
and sauté the chicken until cooked through.

makes 2 portions

MEATY MENUS

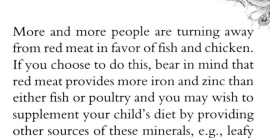

More and more people are turning away from red meat in favor of fish and chicken. If you choose to do this, bear in mind that red meat provides more iron and zinc than either fish or poultry and you may wish to supplement your child's diet by providing other sources of these minerals, e.g., leafy green vegetables, beans and nuts. Meat also contains B vitamins including B_{12}, which is not found in foods of vegetable origin, but is vital for healthy blood and nerves.

I find that children tend to prefer recipes made with ground meat rather than chunks of meat, which are difficult to chew. Make sure that when you buy ground meat, there is very little fat. You can always ask your butcher to grind some lean cuts of beef especially for you. A good tip is to chop the ground meat in a food processor once it has been cooked to make it even softer for your child to chew. If you are making a stew or goulash, trim the meat first to cut away the fat and any tough pieces of tendon, and cook in a slow oven for several hours so that it is tender.

If your child is reluctant to eat meat, then try making a tasty meat and tomato sauce and serve this over pasta. I have found that many children who would not normally touch meat are quite happy to eat it when it is combined with something that they enjoy, like pasta or rice.

Children also love having their own individual portions. If you are making a shepherd's pie for the whole family, reserve a little to make a separate dish for your child. This is much more appetizing than a portion just spooned onto a plate.

succulent leek and meat croquettes

These mini-burgers are soft and juicy. They have a delicious flavor and are very simple to make.

2 leeks, carefully washed
½ lb lean ground beef
Vegetable oil or margarine for sautéing

1 egg, beaten
Salt and freshly ground black pepper
2 tablespoons flour

Discard the roots and tough outer leaves of the leeks and slice into rounds. Cook the leek slices in water until tender (about 30 minutes). Meanwhile sauté the meat in the oil or margarine until browned. Once the meat is cooked, chop it for a few seconds in a food processor to make it softer to chew. Drain the leeks and squeeze out as much water as possible. Mix the leeks with the meat, beaten egg, a little seasoning and finally the flour.

Form into mini-hamburgers or croquettes and either sauté in more oil or margarine, or grill or broil.

makes about 12 croquettes

lamb chops baked in a packet ❈

This is a very easy recipe that seals in all the flavor of the chops. Some children are quite happy chewing meat, especially if they can chew it off a bone. You could also serve the chops with the barbecue sauce on page 93.

¼ small onion, peeled and finely chopped
1 small potato, peeled and cut into small cubes
½ small green pepper, seeded and chopped

Vegetable oil for sautéing
2 lamb rib chops
1 medium tomato, peeled and finely chopped
Salt and freshly ground black pepper
A knob of butter or margarine

Preheat the oven to 350°F.
Sauté the onion, potato and green pepper in vegetable oil. Meanwhile place the chops on a piece of foil. Cover with the sautéed vegetables and chopped tomato. Season lightly with salt and pepper and dot with butter or margarine. Fold the foil around the chops and bake for 1 hour.

makes 2 portions

miniature meatballs

Children love the taste of these tiny meatballs. I stick toothpicks into them and my children love biting them off the sticks. However, make sure you are watching them so that they do not end up poking the sticks into each other! This recipe is good served with rice; meatballs are an excellent standby in your freezer. You can dress them up and serve them mixed with spaghetti in the Tasty tomato sauce for pasta on page 82 or serve them with the sweet and sour sauce from the recipe on page 95.

¼ lbs lean ground beef
1 egg, beaten
2 tablespoons chopped fresh parsley
2 slices whole-wheat bread, made into breadcrumbs
1 onion, peeled and finely chopped

1 garlic clove, crushed (optional)
1 tablespoon tomato purée
1 teaspoon Worcestershire sauce
¼ cup chicken or vegetable stock (see pages 33–34)
Freshly ground black pepper

Preheat the oven to 350°F.
Mix all the ingredients together well, seasoning lightly. Shape into small balls. Place the balls on 2 oiled baking sheets and bake for 20 minutes. Alternatively you can lightly fry the meatballs in vegetable oil until they are browned and then simmer them for 15 minutes in one of the sauces mentioned above.

makes about 50 meatballs

triple-decker shepherd's pie

This recipe makes 6 mini-portions of shepherd's pie, which I freeze and use for a quick ready-made meal. Children love brightly colored peas and sweet corn, which I have used here as the tempting filling between meat and potato (you could also use baked beans). Instead of the cheeses you could use butter or margarine in the mashed potato.

1½ lb lean ground beef
1 small garlic clove, crushed (optional)
Vegetable oil or margarine for sautéing
1 large onion, peeled and chopped
1 green pepper, seeded and chopped
1 red pepper, seeded and chopped
1 cup mushrooms, washed and sliced
1 can (28 oz) tomatoes, chopped
1 beef or chicken stock cube

¾ cup water
A few drops Worcestershire sauce (optional)
6 medium potatoes, peeled and cut into chunks
½ cup grated Cheddar cheese
¼ cup milk
½ cup each mixed peas and sweet corn
¼ cup margarine

Brown the ground beef and garlic (if using) in the vegetable oil or margarine, then chop it for a few seconds in a food processor to make it soft to chew. Meanwhile sauté the onion until soft, then add the green and red peppers and mushrooms and sauté for 3 to 4 minutes. Combine the beef with the onions and peppers and add the chopped tomatoes with their juices. Dissolve the stock cube in the water and add it, together with the Worcestershire sauce, if using. Simmer gently for about 25 minutes.

Meanwhile, steam the potatoes for about 25 minutes or until soft, and cook the peas and sweet corn. Mash the potatoes with the cheese and milk. Preheat the oven to 350°F.

Spread the meat in 6 individual ramekins, cover with a layer of peas and sweet

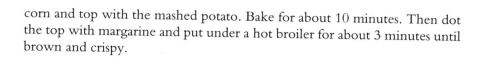

corn and top with the mashed potato. Bake for about 10 minutes. Then dot the top with margarine and put under a hot broiler for about 3 minutes until brown and crispy.

makes 6 portions

Scarlett's tasty rice meal

A complete meal for your child – simple, healthy and very tasty. My two-year-old daughter loves this dish even though she is not keen on eating red meat.

½ cup basmati rice
1¼ cups water
1 onion, peeled and chopped
Vegetable oil for sautéing
½ lb lean ground beef
½ red or green pepper, seeded and chopped
1 tablespoon chopped fresh parsley

1 tablespoon tomato purée
Salt and freshly ground black pepper
2 tomatoes, skinned, seeded and chopped
⅓ cup frozen peas
¾ cup chicken or vegetable stock (see pages 33–34)
½ cup pure apple juice

Cook the rice in the water until tender. Drain well. Sauté the onion in the oil for 2 to 3 minutes. Add the ground beef and cook, stirring, until browned. Add the pepper, parsley, tomato purée and light seasoning and cook for another 3 to 4 minutes. Add the tomatoes, frozen peas, the stock and apple juice; cover and simmer for about 15 minutes. Stir in the cooked rice 5 minutes before the end of the cooking time.

makes 3 portions

Hungarian goulash

The secret of a good Hungarian goulash is to cook for a long time at low heat to ensure that the meat is really tender. It is delicious served with noodles or rice.

Salt and freshly ground black pepper
Flour for coating
1 lb lean braising steak, cut into small cubes
Vegetable oil for sautéing
3 small or 2 large onions, peeled and finely sliced
1 red pepper, seeded and cut into strips
1 green pepper, seeded and cut into strips

1 tablespoon paprika
1 can (28 oz) tomatoes, drained and chopped
2 tablespoons tomato purée
2 tablespoons chopped fresh parsley
1¼ cups chicken, beef or vegetable stock (see pages 33–34)
3 tablespoons sour cream or yogurt

Preheat the oven to 300°F.
Season the flour lightly and roll the beef cubes in it. Sauté them in the oil until browned on all sides. Meanwhile, sauté the onions until soft, add the peppers and cook these for 2 or 3 minutes. Sprinkle with paprika and continue to cook for about 2 minutes.

Put the meat and vegetables into a casserole and add all the remaining ingredients except the sour cream or yogurt. Cover and bake for at least 3 hours, stirring occasionally. Finally stir in the sour cream or yogurt before serving.

makes 6 portions

FRUIT FANTASIES

There is nothing more delicious or better for your child than fresh ripe fruit. It makes great finger food and none of the vitamins and nutrients is destroyed through cooking. My son Nicholas adores fruit so much that we have to hide the fruit bowl until he finishes his main course. Try and encourage your children to eat fruit rather than less healthful sweets.

Present fresh fruit to your child in an appealing way. Make it look attractive; choose contrasting colors of fruit, cut the fruit into interesting shapes and arrange the fruit in patterns on the plate (see illustrations). Always make sure that you remove any seeds or pits before giving fruit to your child – she could so easily choke.

Where raw fruit is concerned, there are endless variations on a theme. Purée or grate fruits and mix them with cottage cheese, yogurt or crème fraîche. Cut the fruit into bite-sized chunks, thread on a skewer to make fruit kebabs and maybe serve with a dipping sauce like yogurt and honey or crème fraîche mixed with fruit purée. Make gelatin desserts (you can make your own with fruit juice and gelatin) and add fresh fruit—berries are good set in raspberry juice. Make a banana sandwich – simply cut a banana in half lengthwise, spread one side with cream cheese and press a layer of granola on top. Cover with the other half of the banana and cut in two. Dried fruits left to soak in boiling water make good finger food, or serve a dried fruit compote with warm custard (see the chapter Scrumptious snacks for more ideas).

Try giving your children other unusual fruits like persimmon, which looks like an orange tomato and tastes a little like a plum. It works well mixed with cottage cheese or yogurt and can be found in large supermarkets when it is in season. Papaya and mango also blend well with dairy products. Kiwi fruit is a good source of vitamin C and makes a good snack peeled and cut into slices. Let your child try the

slightly tart taste of some fruit desserts like apples and blackberries and you may be surprised how much she enjoys them.

On a hot day there is nothing nicer than some Homemade ice pops (see page 115). They are much better for your child than the highly colored, artificially flavored commercial frozen pops.

winter fruit salad

A mixture of various dried fruits – apple rings, dried apricots, prunes and maybe peaches and pears – can be bought in most supermarkets. Add some fresh fruits and maybe some dates, raisins or even toasted pine nuts, or use your child's favorite dried fruits.

1¼ cups mixed dried fruits
¾ cup unsweetened apple or grape juice
¾ cup water
1 apple, peeled, cored and cut into slices
2 oranges, peeled and cut into segments with the pith removed

4 plums, peeled, pitted and cut into slices or 1 large pear, peeled and cut into slices
1 banana, peeled and cut into slices

Simmer the dried fruits in the fruit juice and water for about 10 minutes. Then add the prepared fresh fruit and simmer for another 3 to 4 minutes.

makes 5 portions

apple snowman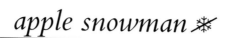

This is a great way to turn a baked apple into a special treat for children.

2 cooking apples, cored
2 tablespoons raisins
1 tablespoon brown sugar
½ teaspoon cinnamon
1 tablespoon butter or margarine
2 teaspoons apricot jam

6 tablespoons water
1 egg white
1 teaspoon sugar
2 blueberries, 2 raisins, 1 strawberry,
1 kiwi fruit for decoration

Preheat the oven to 350°F. With a knife score all the way around the skin of the apple; this will stop the apple skin from bursting in the oven. Stuff the apples with the raisins. Sprinkle with the brown sugar and cinnamon and dot with butter or margarine. Place 1 teaspoon of jam on top of each apple. Put the apples onto an ovenproof dish and pour the water around the base of the apples. Place in oven.

After 15 minutes, whisk the egg white until it stands up in soft peaks. Add the sugar and beat again until stiff (taking care not to overbeat). Put a dollop of the egg white on each of the apples. Baste the apples with the liquid in the bottom of the dish and continue to bake for 30 minutes more. Decorate, using the fruit, with the sliced kiwi fruit as the hat.

makes 2 portions

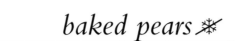

baked pears ❄

A simple but tasty recipe. Instead of fresh pears you could use
a can of pear halves.

4 ripe pears, peeled, cored and halved
Brown sugar

Butter or margarine for dotting
¾ cup yogurt or cream

Preheat the oven to 350°F.
Place the pears hollow side up in a baking dish. Put a little brown sugar inside each pear and top with a knob of butter or margarine (you will need more sugar if using yogurt). Pour the yogurt or cream over the pears and bake for about 10 minutes.

makes 4 portions

cinnamon apple pie

This makes a delicious dessert served hot with ice cream.

¼ cup margarine
⅔ cup brown sugar
1 egg, beaten
1 cup self-rising flour
Pinch of salt
¼ cup milk

2 large cooking apples, peeled and cut
into slices
2 tablespoons raisins
½ teaspoon cinnamon
¼ teaspoon pie spice
1 tablespoon water

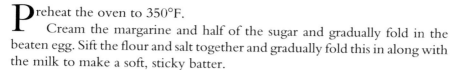

Preheat the oven to 350°F.

Cream the margarine and half of the sugar and gradually fold in the beaten egg. Sift the flour and salt together and gradually fold this in along with the milk to make a soft, sticky batter.

Mix the apple slices with the remaining sugar, raisins, cinnamon and pie spice and cover the base of an 8-inch pie dish. Add the water. Spoon the batter over the apples and spread it as evenly as possible. If there are gaps, you will find that the batter will spread once it is in the oven. Bake for about 40 minutes.

makes 8 portions

triple berry parfait ✳

This is a delicious recipe for berries that aren't quite sweet enough to eat on their own – I serve it in tall glasses and it looks spectacular.

1½ cups blackberries, fresh or frozen
1½ cups raspberries, fresh or frozen
1½ cups strawberries, fresh or frozen

¼ cup sugar
½ cup whipping cream
¾ cup yogurt

Put half the fruit into a saucepan with the sugar and 1 tablespoon of water and simmer for 3 to 4 minutes. Put the cooked berries through a food mill to get rid of the seeds. Beat the cream until thick, stir in the fruit purée when cool (it will turn a wonderful purple color), and swirl in the yogurt. Spoon some of the remaining fresh berry mixture into each glass and mix with enough sugar to sweeten. Top with the yogurt mixture.

makes 4 portions

baked blackened bananas ❄

This is one of my favorite desserts and it's simple to make. Children are fascinated to see the skin of the banana turn black! These are fabulous served hot with vanilla ice cream.

3 large or 4 small bananas
¼ cup unsalted butter or margarine
3 tablespoons brown sugar

½ cup freshly squeezed orange juice
1 tablespoon lemon juice
¼ teaspoon cinnamon

Preheat the oven to 400°F.
Cut a slit lengthwise in the skin of each banana and place on a baking sheet. Bake in the oven for about 15 minutes or until the skins turn black. Meanwhile, melt the butter or margarine over gentle heat and stir in the rest of the ingredients. Bring to a boil and cook for about three minutes, stirring. Peel the cooked bananas and add these to the sauce for 3 to 4 minutes, basting well and turning.

makes 2 portions

homemade ice pops

In summer when your toddler is hot and fussy and off his food, the one thing that will tempt him to eat is ice cream. I find that often what they won't eat on a plate they will eat frozen at the end of a stick. Plastic ice pop molds are inexpensive and available in most supermarkets. Simply pour the mixture into the mold and cover with the top, which is also the stick. Once frozen, run under warm water to remove. These pops are far better than commercial ones filled with artificial coloring and flavorings.

FROZEN BERRY POP
Simmer strawberries or raspberries with a little water and sugar to taste. Put the mixture through a sieve and mix with some apple juice.

RAINBOW POP
This has to be frozen in three stages. You need one layer each of orange juice, apple juice and pineapple juice.

MANGO MUNCHKIN
Blend together 1 container of yogurt, ½ ripe mango and 1 tablespoon maple syrup.

PLUM RIPPLE
Make a plum purée from fresh plums and a little sugar and swirl this into some yogurt.

FRESH FRUIT SALAD POP
Blend together ½ cup freshly squeezed orange juice, 1 pear, 1 peach and 1 small banana.

TROPICANA
Blend together 1 orange (cut in segments with pith removed), 1 peach and 1 mango.

WATERMELON CRUSH
Remove the seeds from chunks of sweet watermelon and blend.

PEANUT BUTTER PARADISE
Mix together peanut butter, softened vanilla ice cream and fresh strawberry purée (simply simmer with a little water and sugar and purée) or strawberry jam.

LOVELY LUNCH BOXES

Reliable surveys show that the diets of many young children are high in fat, sugar and salt and often seriously low in some vitamins and minerals necessary for healthy growth and development. Fewer children are eating school lunches, and the most popular alternative is a packed lunch typically including a sandwich, chips, candy, and a sweet drink. In a recent consumer survey only one in four lunch boxes contained any fruit.

Children don't care how healthy their food is. If it doesn't appeal to them, they won't eat it. Cookie cutters in the shape of toys or animals can transform sandwiches or other foods into delightful treats. Your child will be much more enthusiastic about a teddy bear-shaped sandwich that will arouse a lot of interest from his classmates! Put the food into colorful lunch bags; thread cheese, fruit or vegetables onto skewers (food is much more fun if it can be eaten off a stick); or even draw a face on the skin

of a banana with a felt pen. Touches like these will mean a lot to your child and will encourage her to eat.

With a little imagination, you can pack delicious lunch boxes with lots of variety. Organization is the key and many things can be prepared the day before or even frozen. Last night's dinner is always a good starting point – miniature chicken or fish balls, slices of roast chicken, a stir-fry or a tasty bean stew or hearty soup in a Thermos for cold winter days. To keep a fresh sandwich or salad cool in hot weather, pack it next to a frozen drink.

Let your child help choose what goes into his lunch box and, if you have time, involve him in the preparation. He will be thrilled to just peel an egg or cut shapes out of his sandwiches, using a cookie cutter. There are lots of ideas for sandwich fillings in the chapter Parties and Special Treats. I hope the following list will give you other ideas for your child's lunch box:

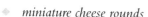

- miniature cheese rounds
- tuna and pasta salad with mayonnaise
- chicken on a stick (page 100). Chicken satay can be bought in supermarkets
- cut an apple in half, scoop out the core, spread the hollow with peanut butter, then put the apple back together again and wrap in foil
- raisins and cashew nuts (give whole nuts only to older children)
- yogurt and crème fraîche
- fruit kebabs made with different fruits
- raw vegetable sticks with a dip (you could use an empty yogurt container for the dip)
- slice of pizza
- rolled-up slices of turkey or chicken, secured with toothpicks
- hard-boiled eggs (slice in half, then mash the egg yolk with cream cheese, chopped liver or creamy salmon, tuna or chicken and wrap in plastic film)
- slices of cheese cut into shapes with cookie cutters
- stuffed pockets: small pita breads stuffed with different fillings are very popular with children. Try canned tuna or salmon mixed with mayonnaise and some chopped green onions or a slice of meat loaf

The following recipes elsewhere in the book also make good lunch box food:
- Chicken and potato pancake (page 94)
- Chicken drumsticks with barbecue sauce (page 93)

- Cheese, onion and tomato tart (page 76)
- Muffin meals (pages 74 and 128)
- Cold chicken with sweet curry sauce with rice (page 98)
- Fish-shaped salmon cakes (page 87)
- Mermaid morsels (page 85)
- Carrot and pineapple muffins (page 137)
- Golden apple and raisin muffins (page 136)
- Blissful banana bread (page 66)
- Tasty tomato soup (page 71)
- Onion soup with floating stars (page 72)
- Ravishing risotto (page 79)
- Mock baked beans (page 49)
- Scarlett's tasty rice meal (page 107)
- Tasty chicken stir-fry (page 92)
- Miniature meatballs (page 105)

chicken sausages

These deliciously moist chicken sausages make excellent finger food eaten cold. They freeze very well. Simply add 3 or 4 to your child's lunch box.

2 boneless chicken breasts
1¼ cups chicken or vegetable stock (see pages 33–34)
1 onion, peeled and finely chopped
1-2 tablespoons butter or margarine
¼ cup flour

¼ cup grated Swiss or Gruyère cheese
Salt and freshly ground black pepper
1 egg, lightly beaten
Flour for coating
Margarine or oil for sautéing

Cut the chicken breasts into pieces and poach in the stock until cooked through (about 10 minutes). Sauté the onion in the butter or margarine and cook very gently for about 6 minutes until soft. Drain the chicken, reserving the stock. Chop the chicken in a food processor, mix with the onions and cook for a few minutes more. Stir in the flour and mix well, then gradually add ⅔ cup of the stock. Cook for several minutes until the mixture thickens, then stir in the cheese and season with a little salt and freshly ground black pepper.

Put the mixture into a bowl and let it cool. Using wet hands, roll the chicken into small sausages; dip into lightly beaten egg and then coat with flour. Sauté in margarine or oil until browned.

makes 10 sausages

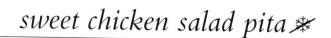

sweet chicken salad pita ✳

⅓ cup cooked chicken, chopped
1 tablespoon grated Gruyère or
Swiss cheese
1 teaspoon finely sliced green onion
(optional)

1 tablespoon drained crushed pineapple
or chopped canned peaches
A little shredded lettuce
1 tablespoon mayonnaise
1 small round pita bread

Simply mix all the ingredients and stuff inside the pita bread.

makes 2 portions

chicken balls with apples and zucchini

Combining chicken with apples brings out a flavor that children love.

2 boneless chicken breasts, cut into
pieces
½ small onion, peeled and grated
1 small zucchini, washed and grated
2 Granny Smith apples, peeled and
grated

Squeeze of lemon juice
4 tablespoons wheat germ
1 chicken stock cube, crumbled
½ beaten egg
Salt and freshly ground black pepper
Vegetable oil for sautéing

Combine all the ingredients together except the last three and chop in a food processor. Add the beaten egg; season and mix well. Form into walnut-sized balls and sauté in vegetable oil until golden brown. Alternatively the balls can be poached in chicken stock or tomato sauce for about 8 minutes.

makes about 15 balls

vermicelli omelette

Children love pasta, and this is a good way of making it part of a lunch box. This recipe uses onion, red pepper and peas, but you could make up your own combination using your child's favorite vegetables. Eat the rest yourself or simply freeze portions so that they are on hand when you need them.

1 small onion, peeled and chopped
½ red pepper, seeded and chopped
Butter or margarine for sautéing
3 oz vermicelli

3 eggs, beaten
Salt and freshly ground black pepper
½ cup frozen peas

Sauté the onion and pepper in butter or margarine until soft. Meanwhile cook the vermicelli in boiling water. When it is ready, drain and chop it.

Season the beaten eggs lightly with salt and pepper and add the onion, pepper, peas, vermicelli and cheese. Melt a tablespoon of butter or margarine in a heavy 8-inch frying pan and tilt the pan so that the sides are coated half way up. Then sauté the egg mixture over gentle heat for about 8 to 10 minutes or until the omelette is lightly browned underneath. To finish, brown under a hot broiler for about 3 minutes.

makes 6 portions

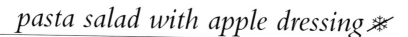

pasta salad with apple dressing ✳

The secret of this recipe is to choose a fun-shaped pasta – I've found animal pasta and spaceship pasta in my local supermarket! If you don't have a steamer, you can use steaming baskets in ordinary saucepans – just start cooking the sweet corn and red pepper 3 minutes later than the broccoli and cauliflower.

5 oz fun-shaped pasta
1 chicken breast
⅔ cup chicken or vegetable stock (see pages 33–34)
½ cup cauliflower florets
½ cup broccoli florets
1 zucchini
½ cup frozen sweet corn

¼ red pepper, seeded and finely chopped
1½ tablespoons balsamic or wine vinegar
2 tablespoons apple juice
2 tablespoons olive oil
Salt and freshly ground black pepper
1 tablespoon chopped green onion or chives

Cook the pasta in boiling water until tender. Cut the chicken breast into small pieces and poach in the stock until cooked through (about 8 minutes). Meanwhile, prepare the vegetables and steam in a two-tiered steamer, broccoli and cauliflower below, zucchini, sweet corn and red pepper on top. Steam for about 6 minutes – vegetables should still be crisp.

To prepare the dressing, whisk the vinegar together with the apple juice, oil and light seasoning, then add the green onion or chives. Combine the cooked, drained pasta with the vegetables and chicken and toss in the dressing.

makes 4 portions

chicken soup with rice and vegetables

I find that children like soups that are full of lots of different ingredients,
and this recipe is a good way to get your child to eat a really healthy meal.
I like to add some mild curry powder to this soup – it is surprising how
many children like the flavor of curry.

2 chicken breasts
8 cups chicken or vegetable stock (see pages 33–34)
1 medium onion, peeled and finely chopped
1 stalk of celery, finely chopped
1 carrot, peeled and finely chopped
Vegetable oil for sautéing

1 cup basmati rice
1 small green pepper, seeded and finely chopped
2 tomatoes, peeled and finely chopped
1 tablespoon mild curry powder
1 tablespoon tomato purée
Salt and freshly ground black pepper

Cook the chicken breasts in the stock for about 20 minutes or until tender.
Sauté the onion, celery and carrot in vegetable oil for about 3 minutes;
add the rice and green pepper and continue to cook for 3 minutes. Add the
tomatoes, curry powder and tomato purée and simmer for a couple of minutes.
Add the vegetables to the chicken stock, lightly season the soup and simmer
for 30 minutes. Remove the skin and bones from the chicken and chop up the
meat. Add the chopped chicken to the soup and simmer for 3 to 4 minutes.

makes about 8 portions

SCRUMPTIOUS SNACKS

If your child eats three good meals a day then you are a very lucky mother indeed. The rest of us need to supplement our child's diet with healthy snacks. Often children just do not have the patience to sit down and eat a proper meal. Little children's stomachs are small and it is difficult for them to eat enough at breakfast to last them until lunchtime when they have been rushing around all morning. Snacks are therefore a very important part of a child's diet.

If you encourage your child when she is very young to enjoy eating healthy snacks like fresh fruit, carrot sticks or slices of cheese instead of bars of chocolate, candy or ice cream, it is likely that she will continue these habits later in life and enjoy a much healthier diet.

Don't forget that many packed snack foods consist mainly of puffed-up, artificially flavored and colored cereals, high in fat and salt, with next to no nutritional value. Many of the additives used are not permitted by law in foods for babies and young children, although the products are made to appeal to young consumers. If you do buy chips, look out for the increasing range of reduced-fat and lightly salted varieties. Even so, these still often contain high levels of salt and fat.

Good snack recipes elsewhere in the book are Carrot and pineapple muffins (page 137), Golden apple and raisin muffins (page 136), Sesame tofu sticks (page 76), Mermaid morsels (page 85), Grandma's chopped liver (page 99), Chicken sausages (page 118), Chicken balls with apples and zucchini (page 119) and Stuffed pockets (page 117).

fruit snacks

When possible, try some exotic fruits like mango, lychees, papaya, persimmons and kiwi fruit (a good source of vitamin C). Mixed berries are also good fruits to try and, if they are not very sweet, add a tiny sprinkling of confectioner's sugar.

A fun way of giving fruit to your child is to pile an assortment of chopped fruits into an ice cream cone; on a hot day put a scoop of vanilla ice cream underneath.

For a special treat, a very appealing way of giving fruit to children is to melt some dark chocolate and some white chocolate in separate pans. Dip the tip of the fruit into the chocolate and pierce the fruit with a toothpick. Insert the toothpicks with the fruit into an orange and put this into the refrigerator to allow the chocolate to harden on the fruit. Strawberries, pineapple chunks and orange or tangerine segments are especially nice but you must eat them the same day. If you are worried about your child having too much chocolate, use carob as a substitute. (Carob has no caffeine in it and it is lower in calories, fat content and salt.) Remember to remove the toothpicks before giving the fruit to very young children.

You can also combine fruit with other healthy foods – for example, cottage cheese with chopped pineapple or a cracker with peanut butter and apple.

caged monsters

These are fun snacks that look wonderful and take only 5 minutes to make. Older children will enjoy making up their own monsters with your help, using whatever ingredients you happen to have (see illustration).

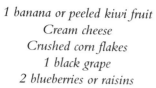

1 banana or peeled kiwi fruit
Cream cheese
Crushed corn flakes
1 black grape
2 blueberries or raisins

1 date or grape
1 large orange
2 teaspoons watercress or sprouts,
chopped
Toothpicks

Peel the banana and cut a 2½-inch chunk from the top of the banana or follow the recipe, using a whole ripe kiwi fruit. Spread some cream cheese over the banana with a knife and roll it in the crushed corn flakes. Cut 2 slices of grape for the eyes, stick these on the banana with a blob of cream cheese and in the center of these, stick on the blueberries or raisins, again using the cream cheese. Stick in a date or grape for a nose.

Cut 2 thick slices from the center of a large orange. Put the monster on top of one of these slices and surround with the watercress or sprouts. Put toothpicks around the edge of this slice to make the "bars" of the cage and then place the other slice so that it is balanced on top of the sticks to form a roof.

Once my children have let the monster out of his cage, I cut the orange slices in half and they can eat these too.

makes 1 caged monster

three blind mice on toast

This fun snack looks like three blind mice hiding under a blanket. It's a great way of getting your child to eat cheese and tomatoes on toast and easy to make.

1 piece of whole-wheat bread
Butter or margarine for spreading
6 cherry tomatoes

2 slices of cheese
Some cooked strands of spaghetti

Toast the bread and spread with butter or margarine, then cut the toast in half. Cut a thin slice off the bottom of the tomatoes so that they stand up. Arrange 3 in a row on the edge of each piece of toast. Put the 2 cheese slices on top of the tomatoes (see illustration).

Place the toast on a plate in the microwave and cook on full power for about 30 seconds or until the cheese has melted. Alternatively, cook under a preheated broiler for about 1 minute or until the cheese melts. Stick a strand of cooked spaghetti under the cheese for the tail.

makes 2 portions

vegetable spaghetti

This never fails to impress! You can add a few chopped herbs if you like.

1 large carrot, peeled
1 large zucchini

Butter or margarine for sautéing

Pare both the carrot and the zucchini into long thin ribbons, using a potato peeler. Melt a little butter or margarine in a frying pan and sauté the vegetable spaghetti for about 3 minutes.

serves 2

fruit kebabs

Children love food on sticks, and for special occasions you can dip the fruit into chocolate. If you are making several kebabs stick them into a large orange or grapefruit. Supervise young children as kebab sticks can be sharp. Make the kebabs from a selection of the following ingredients. Apples and bananas will need to be sprinkled with lemon juice to prevent them from turning brown.

chunks of cheese, chunks of cooked chicken, cherry tomatoes, chunks of cucumber, chunks of apples, grapes,

strawberries, pineapple chunks, melon chunks, chunks of peeled kiwi fruit, chunks of banana, dried fruits

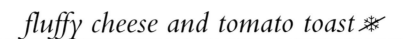

fluffy cheese and tomato toast ❄

This is simple and quick to prepare and so delicious that I can't resist making an extra one for me too! For variation, you can substitute sliced sautéd mushrooms for the tomato.

1 tomato, skinned, seeded and chopped   *⅓ cup grated Cheddar cheese*
1 tablespoon butter or margarine   *2 pieces of whole-grain bread, toasted*
1 egg

Sauté the tomato in the butter for about a minute. Separate the egg and mix together the yolk, the grated cheese and the cooked tomato. Beat the egg white until stiff and fold this into the cheese mixture. Pile onto two slices of toast and place under a preheated broiler until fluffy and golden.

makes 2 portions

Cheddar cheese muffins

For variation, add one large grated carrot or some cooked sweet corn. These freeze well and you can simply take out as many as you need, cover with foil and reheat in the oven.

2 eggs   *1¼ cups flour*
¼ cup vegetable oil   *⅔ cup whole-wheat flour*
½ cup crème fraîche   *1½ teaspoons baking powder*
2 tablespoons maple syrup   *½ teaspoon baking soda*
¾ cup grated Cheddar cheese   *½ teaspoon salt*
1 teaspoon dry mustard

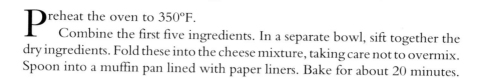

Preheat the oven to 350°F.
Combine the first five ingredients. In a separate bowl, sift together the dry ingredients. Fold these into the cheese mixture, taking care not to overmix. Spoon into a muffin pan lined with paper liners. Bake for about 20 minutes.

makes 12 muffins

Mr. banana face

Rice cakes are popular with children; I think it is the texture they like. Combining a rice cake with this nutritious topping makes an amusing snack.

1 rice cake
Peanut butter, cream cheese or
crème fraîche

Slices of banana
1 cherry tomato
Raisins

Spread the rice cake with some peanut butter or cream cheese or crème fraîche; arrange slices of banana for the eyes, a cherry tomato for the nose and raisins for a smile.

makes 1 portion

animal dips

Tasty dips with raw vegetables, sesame sticks, crackers, chips or parboiled vegetables make a wonderful snack for children of all ages. It's simple to decorate the dips to make them look like animal faces – the color of the dip will give you inspiration: avocado for a frog, peanut for a lion, cream cheese and tomato for a pig (see the illustrations). A few minutes spent on presentation will make all the difference!

Offer your child some of the following for dipping: scrubbed carrot sticks; strips of red, yellow or green pepper; raw cauliflower florets; cucumber sticks; slices of avocado; sticks of celery; cherry tomatoes; radicchio (red lettuce) or chicory.

peanut lion dip ✳

This works with fruit as well as vegetables.

½ cup yogurt
¼ cup cream cheese
¼ cup peanut butter
1 tablespoon maple syrup
Chips, sesame sticks, cooked spaghetti,
strips of yellow pepper or celery

Carrot sticks
1 slice of mushroom
2 olives or 2 bits of cheese
2 blueberries
Red pepper or tomato

S imply mix the yogurt, cream cheese, peanut butter and syrup together and then decorate: make a mane using the chips or one or a combination of the alternatives; whiskers with the carrot sticks; a nose with the mushroom slice, and eyes with the olives or cheese (using the blueberries for the center). Finally place a strip of red pepper or tomato to make a mouth.

makes 1¼ cups

avocado frog dip

You can use slices of cucumber with slices of olive on top for the eyes and strips of chives for the mouth.

1 small avocado
¼ small onion, peeled and finely chopped
¼ small red pepper, seeded and finely chopped

Squeeze of lemon juice
1 tablespoon chopped chives
½ cup cream cheese
Salt and freshly ground black pepper

Cut the avocado in half, remove the pit and scoop out the flesh. Mash or blend all the ingredients together, seasoning lightly.

makes 1¼ cups

lucky dip

A good idea when you are out and about with the children is to make up little snack bags, using brightly colored miniature bags and filling them with lots of different healthy foods. Below are some of the foods you might choose for a healthy alternative to a package of chips.

Miniature cheese rounds, wrapped
Cherry tomatoes
Dried fruits like apple rings, dates, apricots, raisins, banana chips
Carrot, celery or cucumber sticks

Grapes, plums, apple slices
Healthy breakfast cereals
Sesame sticks
Whole-grain foods like unsweetened popcorn and wheat or rye crackers

COOKIES, CAKES AND MUFFINS

So many parents reach for the cookie jar to find their child a between-meal snack. Supermarket shelves offer a tempting array of brightly colored cookies, chocolate-coated teddy bears and jam tarts. These attractively packaged products designed specifically to appeal to children are likely to contain nothing but empty calories and do nothing but harm to your child's diet, spoiling his appetite for more wholesome foods and promoting tooth decay.

Why not make your own delicious home-baked cakes and cookies? At least you will know *exactly* what your child is eating. With a little imagination and some fun-shaped cookie cutters there is no reason why they should not be every bit as appealing to your child as the storebought variety, and there are many recipes in this section that are quick and easy to make. Muffins are very popular with my children – they're full of good wholesome ingredients and my children like the fact that they get their own individual treats.

chewy chocolate oatmeal cookies

Simple to make but hard to resist! You can also make these cookies using white chocolate chips, raisins or chopped dried fruit in place of the chocolate chips.

1 cup butter or margarine
⅓ cup brown sugar
⅓ cup granulated sugar
1 egg
1 tablespoon milk
1 teaspoon vanilla extract
1 cup whole-wheat flour

½ teaspoon baking powder
½ teaspoon baking soda
½ teaspoon salt
¾ cup rolled oats
⅔ cup roughly chopped pecans
¾ cup chocolate chips

Cream the butter or margarine with the sugars. Beat in the egg, milk and vanilla. Sift together the flour, baking powder, baking soda and salt, and beat this into the mixture. Finally stir in the oats, chopped pecans and chocolate chips. Cover and refrigerate the dough for at least 1 hour.

Preheat the oven to 350°F. Line baking sheets with nonstick baking parchment. Form the dough into walnut-sized balls and flatten slightly onto the baking sheets, making sure they are spaced well apart. Bake for 12 to 15 minutes. They will still be quite soft but will harden once they have cooled.

makes about 24 cookies

melt-in-the-mouth whole-wheat cookies

These delicious cookies are full of healthy ingredients even though they
taste sinfully good!

¼ cup butter or margarine
⅓ cup brown sugar
1 egg
½ teaspoon vanilla extract
⅓ cup wheat germ
½ cup rolled oats

⅓ cup whole-wheat flour
½ teaspoon baking powder
¼ teaspoon salt
6 large dates, pitted and chopped
⅓ cup raisins
⅔ cup chopped pecans

Preheat the oven to 350°F.
Cream the butter or margarine together with the sugar. Beat in the egg
and vanilla. In a bowl, mix together the wheat germ, oats, flour, baking
powder and salt. Stir the flour mixture into the butter or margarine mixture
just until blended. Finally fold in the dates, raisins and pecans.

Form into walnut-sized balls and flatten onto baking sheets lined with nonstick baking parchment. Bake for about 10 minutes and cool on a wire rack.

makes about 24 cookies

best-ever oatmeal raisin cookies

These and Chewy chocolate oatmeal cookies (see page 133) are my favorite homemade cookies.

⅓ cup butter or margarine
¼ cup brown sugar
2 tablespoons granulated sugar
½ beaten egg
1 tablespoon water
1 teaspoon vanilla extract
⅓ cup whole-wheat flour

½ teaspoon pie spice
Pinch of salt
¼ teaspoon baking soda
⅔ cup oat flakes or quick-cooking rolled oats
⅓ cup raisins

Preheat the oven to 350°F.
Cream the butter or margarine with the sugars. Beat in the egg and add the water and vanilla. Sift together the flour, pie spice, salt and baking soda. Mix this into the egg mixture. Finally stir in the oats and raisins.

Line baking sheets with nonstick baking parchment. Make walnut-sized balls of dough and flatten these down onto the baking sheet – you may want to enlist the "help" of your child for this stage. Bake for about 15 minutes, until the edges are done but the centers are still soft.

makes about 15 cookies

golden apple and raisin muffins

These delicious muffins are full of goodness and deliciously tempting.
Serve them as a snack for your child at any time during the day.

1 cup flour
1 teaspoon baking powder
2 teaspoons baking soda
⅓ cup brown sugar
¼ teaspoon salt
1 teaspoon cinnamon
¾ cup bran flakes, crushed

1 egg
½ cup milk
½ cup apple juice
⅓ cup vegetable oil
½ cup raisins
⅔ cup chopped pecans or walnuts
1 apple, peeled and grated (optional)

Preheat the oven to 350°F.
In a large bowl, sift together the flour, baking powder, baking soda, brown sugar, salt and cinnamon. Add the crushed bran flakes. In another bowl, beat together the egg, milk, apple juice and vegetable oil. Gradually stir the liquid ingredients into the flour mixture, taking care not to overmix; finally fold in the raisins, nuts and apple, if using.

Line muffin pans with paper liners. Fill each cup about ⅔ full with the batter and bake for about 16 to 20 minutes. The muffins are ready when a toothpick inserted in the center comes out clean.

makes about 10 muffins

carrot and pineapple muffins

These muffins are irresistible – they're my family's favorite snack and are always popular when children come over to play. They can be served plain or iced with cream cheese icing for special occasions.

1 cup flour
1 cup whole-wheat flour
1 teaspoon baking powder
¾ teaspoon baking soda
1½ teaspoons cinnamon
½ teaspoon salt
1 cup vegetable oil

½ cup sugar
2 eggs
2 carrots, grated
1 can (8 oz) crushed
pineapple, drained
⅓ cup chopped pecans
½ cup raisins

Preheat the oven to 350°F.
Sift together the flours, baking powder, baking soda, cinnamon and salt and mix well. Beat the oil, sugar and eggs until well blended. Add the grated carrots, crushed pineapple, pecans, and raisins. Gradually add the flour mixture, beating just enough to combine all the ingredients.

Pour the batter into muffin pans lined with paper liners and bake for 25 minutes.

makes 12–14 muffins

heavenly chocolate mousse cake

This is a good recipe to prepare with your child for a special occasion.

1½ cups graham cracker crumbs
3 tablespoons butter or margarine
¾ cup boiling water
*1 package (2½ oz) lemon gelatin
dessert*

4 oz good-quality chocolate
8 oz cream cheese
⅓ cup sugar
2 eggs, separated
Cocoa powder for decoration

Crush the graham crackers in a food processor. Melt the butter or margarine and stir into the crumbs. Line an 8-inch cake pan with baking parchment and press the crumbs down evenly over the base.

Pour the boiling water over the gelatin and stir until dissolved. Set aside to cool, then refrigerate until it just begins to set. Melt the chocolate and then beat the cream cheese with the sugar, egg yolks and melted chocolate. Whisk the egg whites until stiff. Fold the gelatin mixture into the chocolate mixture together with the egg whites. Pour over the crumb base and put the cake in the refrigerator to set. Sift cocoa powder over the top just before serving.

chocolate peanut butter crisp ❄

This makes a scrumptious treat for lovers of peanut butter. If you prefer, you can leave out the chocolate.

5 tablespoons smooth peanut butter
¼ cup maple syrup
1 teaspoon pure vanilla extract

2 cups rice crispies
4 oz milk chocolate

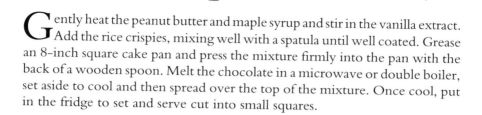

Gently heat the peanut butter and maple syrup and stir in the vanilla extract. Add the rice crispies, mixing well with a spatula until well coated. Grease an 8-inch square cake pan and press the mixture firmly into the pan with the back of a wooden spoon. Melt the chocolate in a microwave or double boiler, set aside to cool and then spread over the top of the mixture. Once cool, put in the fridge to set and serve cut into small squares.

makes 12 squares

apple and date munch and crunch

This is a cross between a pudding and a cake, so you could serve it for parties or after a meal. One thing's for sure, there won't be much left over! It's especially good with fresh dates, which can sometimes be bought in the supermarket.

3 tablespoons butter
⅓ cup brown sugar
1 egg
1 cup whole-wheat self-rising flour
A pinch of salt

1 large cooking apple, peeled, cored and diced
6 dates
⅔ cup chopped pecans or walnuts

Preheat the oven to 350°F.
Beat the butter with the sugar and add the egg. Add the flour and the salt. Fold in the fruit and nuts and spread the mixture in a greased shallow 8-inch square pan. Bake in the oven for about 30 minutes.

makes 6 portions

banana upside-down cake

A lovely moist cake with a delicious topping – cut it into squares and serve
as a special treat.

⅓ cup butter or margarine
½ cup brown sugar
5 bananas, peeled and sliced
½ cup raisins
¾ cup whole pecans, cut into quarters
2 eggs, beaten

1 teaspoon vanilla extract
2 cups self-rising flour
2 teaspoons baking powder
½ teaspoon salt
⅓ cup milk

Preheat the oven to 350°F.
Melt half of the butter or margarine in a saucepan and stir in a third of
the brown sugar until melted. Spread this mixture in a shallow 8-inch square
nonstick cake pan. Arrange the sliced bananas, raisins and pecans on top.

Cream together the remaining butter or margarine and sugar. Beat in
the eggs and vanilla. Sift together the
dry ingredients and gradually beat
these into the first mixture alternately
with the milk until smooth. Pour the
batter over the bananas; don't worry
if there are some gaps as the batter will
spread when cooked.

Bake for 40 to 45 minutes. Remove
from pan while still warm.

makes 12 portions

PARTIES AND SPECIAL TREATS

Amazing isn't it that when we celebrate a happy event, such as a birthday or party, we often serve unhealthy food – hot dogs, chips and cakes with colored icing? Parents are trying against considerable odds to prevent their children from getting a taste for food that undermines their health. Why do "bad" foods always have to be treats; why not "good" foods for a change?

It is much more satisfying seeing children eat with relish a selection of homemade goodies. Your child will enjoy eating the food all the more if you allow her to "help" you make it in the kitchen. Just remember it will probably take you twice as long!

Organization is obviously very important and it's possible to make and freeze most of the cookies and cakes so that you can limit your work on the day of the party. All that you should then need to do is make the sandwiches, frost the cake, set the table and blow up the balloons.

Presentation is important; you can have a lot of fun designing novelty sandwiches, and there are lots of ideas for fun-shaped party food like gelatin boats and animal dips (see pages 147 and 129) that are simple to make. You can cut a watermelon into the shape of an animal and fill it with fruit (see illustration). Scale everything down because children love miniature food and they like to try lots of different things! Make mini-muffins and cookies (see pages 133 to 137) and miniature sandwiches.

With a little imagination, sandwiches can be just as appealing to your child as cookies and ice cream. Sandwiches can make a quick, easy meal for your child. There are so many different breads available in super-markets now – sourdough bread, walnut bread, rye bread – they almost fill the whole aisle. There are all sorts of homemade fillings you can try. It is surprising what a child will eat inside a fancy-shaped sand-wich that she would never touch if it was served to her on a plate!

It's a lot of fun designing sandwiches in all shapes and sizes. Cookie cutters are a very simple way of transforming a simple sandwich into something special for your child. Small animal-shaped cookie cutters are always popular, and you can give the animals eyes, whiskers and tails, where appropriate, using raisins, carrots, cucumber or whatever else comes to mind. Larger cookie cutters like those used to make gingerbread people are great for open-face sandwiches.

Even those parents with limited artistic flair can try their hand at novelty sandwiches. A long train with several cars behind can look spectacular. Just build up a multi-layered sandwich for the steam engine with a chunk of celery for a smokestack and sliced peppers for the wheels. Following behind could be single-layered sandwiches with small chunks of cheese, cucumber and tomato and thinly sliced radishes for the wheels. Add a railway track made from twigs and you are all set.

The fish sandwich in the illustration uses a long whole-grain roll and I have cut a slit in the top where cucumber slices form fins. The blueberries are secured with toothpicks – so remove them before giving to young children.

How about traffic-light sandwiches: Simply trim off the crusts, cut the bread in half and spread with butter or cream cheese. Put a slice of tomato at the top, a slice of hard-boiled egg in the middle and a slice of cucumber at the bottom.

Another idea is to cut out circles of bread using round metal cutters and make open-face sandwiches that look like faces. Spread with a smooth filling or cut out a round piece of cheese, use grated carrot or salad cress for the hair, sliced grape or carrot for the eyes, sliced mushroom for the nose and a sliver of red pepper for the mouth.

patchwork quilt

This is an attractive way of displaying miniature sandwiches – choose toppings of contrasting colors. There are lots of different foods you can use for decoration. This looks great for a special tea party and children will be able to choose their favorite sandwich from the patchwork quilt. Ask them if they know what each sandwich is made from! Alternatively, you can make a patchwork quilt on one slice of bread (see illustration). Cut contrasting colored cheese slices (e.g., Swiss and Cheddar) into squares. Arrange like a chess board on top of the bread and decorate.

4 pieces whole-grain bread
Butter or margarine for spreading
A variety of different toppings – peanut butter, different colored cheeses,

egg salad, etc.
Grapes, sliced cherry tomatoes, cucumber, radishes, lettuce, etc. for decoration

Spread the slices of bread with butter or margarine. Remove the crusts and cut each slice into strips. Put a different topping on each strip and then cut each strip into small squares from each slice of bread. On a large plate, arrange the small squares in rows, varying the different toppings, to make one large square. Decorate some of the squares.

makes 36 miniature open-face sandwiches

tractor-trailer sandwich

This makes a great centerpiece for a birthday party and never fails to impress (see the illustration). Simply layer brown and white bread and spread with different but complementary fillings like egg, cream cheese, cucumber, tomato and so on and form into the shape of a truck. Make the trailer from one and a half bagels, and some fresh farm produce like cherry tomatoes, cucumber and celery. Make the wheels from sliced red peppers and carrot slices, the windows from cheese slices and chives and a sesame stick for the smokestack. The children will have a great time taking it apart!

multi-layered sandwiches

Layer 3 or 4 slices of bread together with 1 or 2 different fillings. Use brown or white bread or mix them. Cut the bread into fingers, small squares or miniature triangles. Make sure the 2 fillings are complementary!

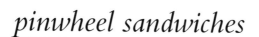

pinwheel sandwiches

These are fun to make and can be frozen in long rolls before they are sliced and wrapped in plastic film. Use a denser bread and if you can, chill it first; this will make it easier to handle. Remove the crusts from 2 slices of bread; lay them on a board so that the edges overlap by about ½ inch. Flatten them so that the bread becomes pliable and the 2 pieces are firmly joined together. Butter the bread and spread with your desired filling. Fillings that contrast with the color of the bread look best. Then carefully roll up the bread along its longest edge. Below is a list of suggested fillings that work well with pinwheel sandwiches.

peanut butter
peanut butter and jam
smooth egg salad with chopped chives or sprouts

smoked salmon
tuna salad
chopped spinach, cream cheese, finely grated Parmesan and a little nutmeg

toasted sandwiches

Miniature toasted sandwiches are very tempting. Cook the open sandwiches under a hot broiler for about 5 minutes. Below are some suggested toppings for you to try.

cheese, tomato and chopped chives
homemade pizza topping – chopped and sautéed tomato, green onion and mushroom with some sliced Mozzarella cheese on top

cooked chopped chicken with sautéed mushrooms in a cream sauce
sliced apple and banana, sprinkled with some brown sugar and cinnamon
tuna, sweet corn and melted cheese

more ideas for sandwiches and fillings

To stop the bread from getting soggy, put lettuce leaves between the bread
and the filling. Bread doesn't always need to be buttered – you can
sometimes use crème fraîche, cottage cheese, or cream cheese or peanut
butter instead.

mashed avocado and cream cheese

*finely chopped chicken with cottage
cheese and chutney*

peanut butter and raspberry jam

*peanut butter and mashed banana with
alfalfa sprouts*

*peanut butter and apple purée with
raisins (and maybe a pinch of cinnamon)*

*peanut butter, grated apple and toasted
sesame seeds*

Cheddar cheese and shredded lettuce

*cream cheese, cucumber and toasted
sesame seeds*

*chopped hard-boiled eggs, sprouts and
mayonnaise*

cream cheese and chopped, peeled grapes

cream cheese and crushed pineapple

mashed sardines

crème fraîche and raisins

grated cheese with grated apple and pear

*canned salmon, chopped egg and
mayonnaise*

tuna salad and sprouts or green onion

*raisin bread with cream cheese and
strawberry jam*

*bagel with cream cheese and slices of
smoked salmon*

cottage cheese with ripe kiwi fruit slices

*chopped chicken, mayonnaise and
yogurt with a little curry powder and
raisins*

*prawns with shredded lettuce, tomato,
cucumber and mayonnaise*

*grilled chicken livers mashed with
sautéed onions and hard-boiled egg*

*egg salad with ½ teaspoon of curry
powder*

*cream cheese with chopped dates, prunes
or dried apricots*

cold chicken or turkey with fruit chutney

cream cheese with fruit purée

*chopped hard-boiled eggs with mashed
sardines*

grated Cheddar, carrot and mayonnaise

yummy gelatin boats

These gelatin boats are irresistible. You can use packages of fruit gelatin or make your own from fruit juices. Try apple, grape or orange juice; you may need to add a little honey or sugar. Another idea is to make lime, orange or peach, and strawberry or raspberry gelatin and set them one after the other in 3 layers. You end up with traffic light gelatin!

2 large oranges
2 teaspoons unflavored gelatin
1 cup fruit juice

2 tablespoons sliced fruit – strawberries,
raspberries, grapes, banana
1 sheet of parchment paper
8 toothpicks

Cut the oranges in half. Squeeze out the juice without breaking the skin and carefully scrape out the pith and discard it (reserve the skins). Heat a little of the fruit juice in a saucepan, add the gelatin and stir, making sure it dissolves completely. Stir in the rest of the fruit juice.

Fill each orange half with the gelatin mixture and add some of the prepared fruit. Make sure that the oranges are filled right to the top. Refrigerate until set and cut the oranges in half again (using a wet blade). Cut triangles out of the parchment paper and secure with toothpicks to make sails.

makes 8 boats

peach and apricot cottage cheesecake

This cake is simple to make, uses no cream, requires no baking and looks very impressive. A lovely cake to make for a special party, it also freezes very well so that you can make it in advance.

1 can (28 oz) apricots
2 packages (5 oz each) peach gelatin dessert
3 cups cottage cheese
1¼ cups crème fraîche

1 package (10 oz) gingersnaps
⅓ cup butter or margarine, melted
1 can (14 oz) apricots
3 tablespoons apricot jam, sieved
A little grated chocolate (optional)

Drain the large can of apricots and reserve 8 tablespoons of syrup. Dissolve the gelatin in this syrup in the top of a double boiler (or use an ordinary saucepan on top of a saucepan containing simmering water) and let cool. Put the cottage cheese through a food mill to make a smooth texture. Put the drained apricots into the food mill to make a purée and stir these into the cottage cheese. Stir in the cooled gelatin mixture and the crème fraîche.

Crush the gingersnaps in a food processor and stir in the melted butter or margarine. Press the crushed cookies onto the base of a 10-inch round cake pan and pour in the apricot cheese mixture.

Place the cake in a refrigerator until set and then decorate with the drained apricot halves from the remaining can of apricots. Dissolve the apricot jam in 1 tablespoon of water and brush this glaze over the top of the cake. You can decorate the cake with a little grated chocolate if you wish.

makes 10 portions

HEALTHY FAST FOOD

Kids love fast food but fast food doesn't love kids! If you ask children to name their favorite foods, fries, hamburgers and ice cream would almost certainly top the list. Fast food companies are directly targeting young children, who are most in need of a diet rich in minerals and vitamins to fuel their growing bodies, and children are faced with a limited range of foods, mainly highly processed and fried. Of course, the occasional visit to the drive-through will do your child no harm, and a dinner of fish sticks and fries when you have all had a busy day makes life nice and easy.

However, fast food on a regular basis is not a good idea. There is no law that obliges fast food companies to declare the ingredients of their products. Underneath the salt, monosodium glutamate, the coloring and the "tasty" breadcrumbs and batters often lurk inferior products like reconstituted fish or fatty ground meat. When it comes to dessert, manufacturers know that the sweeter the product, the more it will appeal; the problem is that this intense sweetness becomes a learned habit and it can be hard to interest children in more natural, healthier foods.

A typical meal of hamburger, fries, apple pie and soda might well represent over 1200 calories, over two thirds of the daily calorie needs of a child between the ages of 4 and 6, and over half the daily calorie needs of an 11- to 14-year-old. However, this meal has a high proportion of saturated fat, salt and sugar but a low level of nutrients for the calories provided. The growing consumption of fast food can lead to an increased incidence of heart disease, obesity and tooth decay, and you may well end up with an overweight, unhappy child. The trouble is, we allow children choice before they have the ability to make informed decisions.

Not all fast food is bad for you. Baked beans on toast makes a great snack, and some fish sticks and hamburgers are made with good-quality ingredients. Give your child a healthier diet by following some of the tips below.

◆ When making fries, cut them thick to absorb less fat. Fry them in canola, safflower or corn oil and drain on paper towels before serving. Better still, offer a baked potato with an interesting topping.

◆ Grill hamburgers (choose a low-fat burger if possible) and serve with a whole-wheat bun.

◆ Choose whole-wheat pizzas.

◆ Frozen vegetables, canned fish and canned beans are all good convenience foods to keep on hand.

◆ Buy canned fruits in natural juices rather than sugary syrups.

◆ Choose ice creams made from good natural ingredients and make your own ice pops from fruit juices (see page 115).

◆ Beware of many "healthy" snacks like granola bars that are often laden with sugar and fat − read the labels carefully.

There are lots of recipes in this section combining "fast food" with other healthy ingredients to make complete meals, e.g., Minestrone with spaghetti stars or Chicken nuggets with potato chips. I have also made up my own healthy fast food recipes for all-time favorites like Pasta pizza and Funny face burgers to entice those fast food junkies back to home cooking!

minestrone with spaghetti stars

Minestrone soup is very popular with children; they love to see all the "bits" floating around. Combine it with a package of tiny pasta "stars" (or even canned spaghetti) and you are on to a real winner.

2 onions, peeled and chopped
Vegetable oil for sautéing
1½ stalks celery, diced
2 carrots, peeled and grated
1½ cups shredded cabbage
12 cups chicken or vegetable stock (see pages 33–34)

2 tablespoons tomato purée
1½ cups frozen peas
1½–2 cups tiny pasta "stars," cooked and drained or 1 can spaghetti
Salt and freshly ground black pepper
Grated Parmesan cheese (optional)

Sauté the onions for 2 minutes in the oil, then add the celery, carrots and cabbage and sauté for a couple of minutes. In a separate pan, bring the stock to a boil and add the sautéed vegetables and tomato purée and simmer for about 10 minutes. Finally, add the peas and pasta. Simmer for about 6 minutes; season with a little salt and pepper and serve. If you wish you can sprinkle some Parmesan cheese on top before serving.

makes about 12 portions

chicken nuggets with potato chips

I make these with crushed cheese and onion chips but you could try other flavors. Choose a good-quality chip without artificial flavors and colorings.

1 small bag cheese and onion chips
1 slice of whole-wheat bread
1 egg
2 teaspoons water
Freshly ground black pepper

Flour for coating
1 large boneless chicken breast, cut into
8 pieces
Vegetable oil

Chop the bread and chips in a food processor to the consistency of fine crumbs. Beat together the egg, water and black pepper in a shallow dish. Spread the flour in a second shallow dish and in a third dish, spread the mixture of chips and breadcrumbs. Dip the chicken pieces first into the flour and then into the egg, letting the excess egg drip back into the dish. Finally, dip the chicken into the crumbs. Either sauté in oil for about 5 minutes or drizzle with a little oil and cook under a preheated broiler for 10 to 15 minutes, or until cooked, turning halfway through.

makes 2 portions

pasta pizza ✳

Pizza with a spaghetti base – two favorites in one meal! Try this tasty cheese, mushroom and tomato topping and then add extra toppings that your child enjoys, like sweet corn or salami, and you can have fun decorating the pizza to look like faces.

6 oz spaghetti
½ teaspoon salt
2 eggs, lightly beaten
½ cup milk
¾ cup grated Gruyère or Swiss cheese
¼ cup grated Cheddar cheese
A little freshly ground black pepper
2 green onions, chopped
10 button mushrooms, sliced
2 tablespoons butter or margarine

5 tomatoes, skinned, seeded and
chopped or 2 cans (14 oz each)
tomatoes, drained and chopped
¼ cup tomato purée
1 tablespoon chopped basil
1 teaspoon oregano
1 cup grated Mozzarella cheese
⅓ cup grated Parmesan cheese
(optional)

Boil the pasta in salted water (leave it a little undercooked as it will be cooked again in the oven). Drain and rinse under water. With a fork, beat together the eggs, milk and half of the Gruyère or Swiss cheese and the Cheddar. Season with a little pepper. Stir this into the pasta. Line a baking sheet with nonstick parchment paper and divide the spaghetti into 3 or 4 circles to form the base of the pizzas.

Preheat the oven to 350°F. Sauté the green onions and the mushrooms in the butter or margarine for a couple of minutes, then add the chopped tomatoes. Simmer for 4 to 5 minutes and stir in the tomato purée, basil and oregano. Continue to simmer for 3 to 4 minutes. Spread the tomato sauce over the pizza bases and sprinkle with the remaining Gruyère or Swiss, the Mozzarella and Parmesan (if using). Bake for 15 to 20 minutes.

makes 3 or 4 individual pizzas

Annabel's baked pizza sandwich

This uses slices of bread instead of pizza dough. It's very simple to make and gets wolfed down by my three children, but there's none left for seconds because Mom usually can't resist helping herself to the fourth portion. You can add some lightly sautéed mushrooms or chopped peppers to the tomato sauce if you like.

1 onion, peeled and chopped
Olive oil for sautéing
1 can (8 oz) chopped tomatoes
2 medium tomatoes, skinned, seeded and chopped
1 teaspoon sugar
1 teaspoon fresh parsley, chopped
½ teaspoon oregano
½ teaspoon dried basil or 1 tablespoon fresh basil

A little salt and freshly ground black pepper
6 large slices whole-grain bread
1 cup milk
1¼ cups grated Mozzarella cheese
¼ cup grated Parmesan cheese
2 eggs
A knob of butter

Preheat the oven to 350°F.
Sauté the onion in the oil until soft, then add the chopped tomatoes, fresh tomatoes, sugar, parsley, oregano and basil. Simmer for about 15 minutes and season with salt and pepper. Meanwhile, soak the bread in the milk for 10 to 15 minutes. Arrange two whole and two half slices of bread on the base of an 8- × 10-inch ovenproof dish; cover with half of the tomato sauce and top with the Mozzarella cheese. Arrange a second layer of bread slices on top and cover with the rest of the tomato sauce. Beat the egg together with the Parmesan, pour this over the top, dot with butter and prick through the layers with a fork. Bake in the oven for 45 minutes.

makes 4 portions

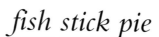

fish stick pie

Some children are confirmed fish haters but will eat fish sticks so this is a quick and easy way to turn fish sticks into a tasty meal. It's simple to make your own delicious fish sticks – cut a thick fillet of haddock or cod into strips, dip in lightly seasoned beaten egg, then roll in flour and coat in crushed corn flakes. Lightly sauté or broil (brushed with melted butter or margarine).

8 fish sticks
1 small onion, peeled and chopped
1 small green pepper, seeded and chopped
1 tablespoon vegetable oil

1 can(14 oz) tomatoes or 4 medium tomatoes, skinned, de-seeded and chopped
1 tablespoon tomato purée
¾ cup grated Cheddar cheese

Grill or sauté the fish sticks until they are cooked. Sauté the onion and green pepper in the oil until soft. Drain the tomatoes, roughly chop them and add to the onion and pepper together with the tomato purée and cook for about 5 minutes. Meanwhile, preheat the oven to 350°F.

Cut the cooked fish sticks into pieces and mix with the tomato sauce. Place in a greased ovenproof dish and cover with the grated Cheddar. Reheat in the oven and finish off under the broiler.

makes 3 portions

funny face burgers

These are great for a barbecue. You can make each one look different (see illustrations). Alternatively, they could be grilled or sautéed, served plain or in a bun with some sautéed onions. I usually make more than I need and put some aside in the freezer (best frozen uncooked and without decoration).

1 large potato, peeled and grated
1 lb lean ground beef
1 onion, peeled and grated
1 Granny Smith apple, peeled and grated
1 tablespoon chopped fresh parsley
1 chicken stock cube

1 bread roll, made into breadcrumbs
Mozzarella cheese for the face, grated
Cheddar cheese, grated, for the hair
Olives or cherry tomatoes or cucumber slices for the eyes
Red pepper for the mouth

Squeeze out the excess liquid from the potatoes. Then mix all the ingredients except the cheeses, olives and pepper together and form into burgers. Barbecue, broil or sauté until cooked through. Sprinkle with some Mozzarella for the face and Cheddar for hair and place under a hot broiler until the cheese melts. Then use the olives etc. to make the faces.

makes about 10 burgers

INDEX

ACKNOWLEDGMENTS

Dr. Margaret Lawson, Head of Dietetics and Senior Lecturer in Pediatric Nutrition at Great Ormond Street Hospital, London, and consultant nutritionist for this book, for her enthusiasm in checking through all my recipes and answering my many queries.

Dr. Alan Lucas MB, B. Chir., MA, MD, FRCP, one of the leading experts in child nutrition, for all his help and advice.

Dr. Barry Scheer, Pediatric Dentist.

Dr. Barry Lewis, FRCP, DCH, Consultant Pediatrician.

Dr. Sam Tucker FRCP, Consultant Pediatrician.

Dr. Jonathan Brostoff, an international authority on food allergies and intolerance.

Suzanne Webber and Nicky Copeland at BBC Books.

Annette Peppis and Susan Martineau.

David Karmel, the computer wizard of the family, for all his advice.

Beryl Lewsey, for all her support and enthusiasm.

Marina and Letty, for helping me with my experiments in the kitchen.

Helen Cox, nutritional therapist.

Andrew and Angela Etkind.

My mother, Evelyn Etkind, for her "unbiased" views on my experiments in the kitchen.

Dr Irving Etkind, for his help in research.

Tom Williams, school caterer at St Paul's Girls School for Gardner Merchant.

Many thanks to Nicholas, Lara, Scarlett and all the babies and children who were "guinea-pigs" to my successes and failures.

Most important of all my husband, Simon, the ultimate connoisseur of food for children, for all his encouragement.